A Heart of Compassion

A Heart
of Compassion

Philip Clarke

Authentic

LONDON • COLORADO SPRINGS • HYDERABAD

First published 2006 by Authentic Media
9 Holdom Avenue, Bletchley, Milton Keynes, Bucks, MK1 1QR, UK
and
1820 Jet Stream Drive, Colorado Springs, CO 80921, USA
OM Authentic Media, Medchal Road, Jeedimetla Village,
Secunderabad 500 055, A.P., India

www.authenticmedia.co.uk

Authentic Media is a division of IBS-STL UK,
a company limited by guarantee (registered charity no. 270162)

British Library Cataloguing in Publication Data
A catalogue record for this book is available from the
British Library

ISBN-13 978-1-85078-663-4
ISBN-10 1-85078-663-1

Cover design by Moose77
Typeset by Waverley Typesetters, Little Walsingham, Norfolk
Print Management by Adare Carwin
Printed in Great Britain by J.H. Haynes & Co., Sparkford

David Anthony 1951–1970

Contents

Contents

Acknowledgements

There are many people who have helped me in the writing of this book, without whom I could not have completed this project. It is impossible to name them all, but it is appropriate to mention a few.

I am indebted to my daughter Rebekah, who has been my editor-in-chief; without her writing and creative skills, the book would have been barely readable! Susan Hutchinson, a close neighbour and a friend from our days at university, has greatly helped in correcting my grammar!

Charlotte Hubback has provided the final editorial oversight and has guided me through the publishing process.

Christine Cook, the longest serving member of our typing team in the medical practice, typed the original manuscript.

I am grateful to my wife Sheelagh, and to Joanna Thompson and the support group within CARE Centres Network, who have been so encouraging in their comments.

It is impossible to name patients, clients and friends, who have allowed their stories to be told, but without them this book would have been pointless. I thank them all for their kindness in allowing me to write about them, and for their courage in baring their souls. They have enriched my life, and I trust that through this book, they will enrich yours.

Finally, a special mention of the bougainvillaea in our conservatory, the significance of which is known only to my family.

Foreword

This book comes from the heart of a compassionate man. I have known Phil and Sheelagh for twenty years and deeply admire the way they have consistently pursued their passion for justice and their concern for social action and care in the community worked out in and through the local church.

In John's gospel, Jesus is described as being 'full of grace and truth' and Phil passionately practises both. The book advocates the growing need to demonstrate his grace first and then earn the right to speak out the truth. Phil brings together helpful biblical teaching on what it means to put gospel grace and truth into practice. He shares challenging and moving real-life stories and comments with deep insight. He has a wealth of experience and wisdom, both as a GP and as a result of his involvement in the wider community. He is a founder of CARE Centres Network and CARE is privileged to partner with this unique nationwide ministry and the CAREconfidential telephone helpline, which has resulted in caring Christians coming alongside thousands of women facing unplanned pregnancies and the aftermath of abortion. Phil Clarke is a true father figure to the movement. Although this book is set in the context of Phil's experience of abortion, its heart encompasses so many more moral and social issues. It's a book about how to make a real difference in our world and I highly recommend it to you.

I pray that reading *A Heart of Compassion* will inspire you and thousands more increasingly to exercise a ministry of mercy to those who most need it.

Lyndon Bowring, CARE

Introduction

If someone had said to me as a boy that one day I would write a book, I would have laughed. Coming near the bottom of the class in English was a perennial problem for me. I just scraped through English O level. I hated writing essays. The sciences were far more exciting, and the fascination of the natural world eventually led me into medicine. It is, therefore, with some trepidation that I come to this point, and yet I feel compelled. Four years ago, within the space of a couple of months, four separate people came to me with the same question. Had I thought of writing a book? Was this coincidence, or was this a reflection of God's heart?

For the past 22 years, I have worked in general medical practice in Southampton. Over the past 18 years, my wife Sheelagh and I have been involved in Crisis Pregnancy Centres. Throughout the development of the work, we have been a part of Southampton Community Church. *A Heart of Compassion* aims to relate our journey thus far, to explain how we have been challenged by the call to social action in the church, confronted by the issue of abortion and humbled by the gospel of mercy, compassion and grace. It is a journey that leads us to the heart of God, to the place of intimacy that he longs to share with us.

Although much of the book relates our experience through the work of pregnancy counselling centres, this is not a book about abortion. I hope it will be read by all who desire to outwork their Christian lives in a practical way and, in so doing, to discover the passionate, gracious and loving heart of the Father. The book contains the stories of many people whose lives have profoundly touched ours. In order to preserve their anonymity, I have changed their names. I have also taken the liberty of changing the *detail* of the story, so as to protect them further, whilst still maintaining the truth of what we have learned from them. Where people have been identified, it has been with their expressed permission. Unless referenced, the Bible quotes are from the Revised Standard Version.

Prologue

Emma's Story

My Child

Emma was the perfect image of her mother, except for her dad's round nose that gave her that 'look at me' quality of youth.

My perfect child. Radiant, beautiful, full of life. She had lived a thousand lives in her eighteen years and her sadness gave her shoulders a slightly hunched appearance. Underneath her confident swagger I saw her hurt, bruised heart, and longed to reach out to her and heal her broken past.

Experience dulled her complexion, but I could always see that light of life glimmering behind the façade that protected her from the world.

I ached for her. For her to feel loved. And yet in my eyes she, that broken human being, was never more or less than my child, whom I loved.

My Patient

Emma had the straggly, mud-blonde hair of her depressed, down-trodden mother. Her appearance

xvi   *A Heart of Compassion*

made me want to turn away and wish for the next patient.

Her prostitution saddened me. It almost made me feel dirty. I couldn't see past the short skirt and provocative look she flashed the guy in the waiting room as she sauntered in. She seemed to be on show, and yet had a slightly worn look of someone who hadn't slept properly for a couple of days. She was only eighteen, but looked about twenty-eight. She should have been at college, I thought.

It was hard to have sympathy for her. After all, she had chosen this degrading life for herself. What had I to offer her? All I felt I could do was to try to point out that what she was doing could lead to all sorts of medical complications in later life.

Emma

I saw the look he shot me when I walked through the door. He looked as though my very presence was dirtying the air around him and I realised he was just like all the other men in my life. Just saw me as a cheap, worthless whore.

But he didn't know what had happened to me, that my childhood had been so horrible. My dad used me for sex because my mum was always depressed, and then, when I cried for help, I was taken away from them. And yet my doctor saw this situation as my fault.

All I wanted was for him to listen. To look past what he saw and understand how desperate I felt, searching for a way out, for a different kind of life. What I really longed for was to be loved and accepted just like anyone else. I just couldn't imagine what it might be like. Rather than seeing me, he just saw what I did, and that seemed to disgust him.

Three perspectives of the same broken human being. A pretty, young, beloved child of God; a dirty, cheap patient of a doctor who felt he had nothing to give. A girl who craved acceptance and love, and found none.

Throughout my life I have often found myself adopting the view of the doctor. It is so easy to judge people, to feel angry, disgusted and frustrated about their life choices. At times even Christians display this kind of judgement. Lack of respect, immoral behaviour, or ungodliness all lead us to label people and make a judgement about their lives.

The woman caught in adultery in the Bible was condemned by everyone who saw her. People were disgusted when she was dragged before Jesus, having been found committing adultery. I might have been one of those people. And yet Jesus chose not to look at her with shame. Instead, he averted his eyes and showed her the kind of love and acceptance that she found nowhere else.

I am very familiar with this Bible story. Yet in life, isn't it easy to react in the same way? The doctor's view in Emma's story, based on a real encounter in my surgery, is representative of how society might perceive this prostitute. Indeed, at times throughout my life I have found myself thinking, feeling and acting very differently to the example set by Jesus, and it wasn't until God began to challenge my reactions to people, to try and see them through his eyes, that I started to change. This was my journey to understanding God's heart of compassion. This book is about my journey.

> *The Spirit of the Lord God is upon me, because the Lord has anointed me to bring good tidings to the afflicted; he has sent me to bind up the brokenhearted, to proclaim liberty to captives, and the opening of the prison to those who are bound; to proclaim the year of the Lord's favour and the day of vengeance of our God; to comfort all who mourn; to grant those who mourn in Zion – to give them a garland instead of ashes, the oil of gladness instead of mourning, the mantle of praise instead of a faint spirit; that they may be called oaks of righteousness, the planting of the Lord, that He may be glorified.*
>
> *Isaiah 61:1–3*

In the midst of a fallen and degenerate society God's heart of love reaches down to those who are in distress. When Jesus took these words to himself (Lk. 4:18), he called his church to not only speak words of life and hope, but through their deeds and through their actions to demonstrate his love, kindness, compassion and mercy to those who are lost.

1

The Journey

Whilst studying for my medical degree, I decided two things. Firstly, I would never stay in my university town of Southampton once I qualified and secondly I would never do psychiatry or General Practice as a career. These decisions taught me a very clear lesson; never say never with God. Throughout my early career God continually showed me that my plans were not necessarily his plans. He also showed me that when things felt hopeless he had everything under control.

I had arrived in Southampton in 1971 to join the first intake of the new medical school. It was a bit of a shock to be so far south when my roots were in the Midlands, where I loved the friendliness and familiarity of my home town of Lincoln. Although my childhood was not unhappy, I never really enjoyed school, the pressure to achieve weighed heavily on me. I would like to say that I chose medicine for grand and altruistic reasons but this was not so. I had no medical heritage in my family. Since I was burdened with the common desire to be loved and wanted, medicine served my insecurities well. Looking back now, the fact that I made it to medical school was a miracle. When I first sat my A levels, I failed them miserably, but I was able to re-sit and just made the grade.

I was determined that my faith would remain strong when I came to university but I found the distractions of the first year quite difficult. Early in my second year, however, I was visited in hall by a group called the Navigators and was encouraged to attend their meetings. The help I received from them at this time was just what I needed to encourage my faith and I started attending a Baptist Church in Southampton where I was subsequently baptised. Through the Navigators I also began to meet other Christians at university. At that time in the early 1970s in Southampton, God was doing amazing things on the campus. A group of Christian students were inspired to establish the Southampton Christian Fellowship, later to become Southampton Community Church.

My first term at medical school was a bit disastrous. The freedom of being away from home meant I did little study and I failed almost all the coursework. However I soon knuckled down and my progress through medical school ran more smoothly, a mixture of very hard work and great fun. Towards the end of my medical school career, with a new church in Southampton having just started, I began to realise that God wanted me to stay in Southampton. This was reinforced by the fact that in my third year of university, I met Sheelagh, who is now my wife. Our early relationship was fairly difficult as we were constantly apart. While she finished her nursing degree in London, I spent two months working in a hospital in Iran, returning to complete my degree in Southampton. Despite these challenges it was incredibly exciting being part of a new vibrant church, and this led us both to realise that our place was in Southampton sharing our lives and living out our faith with the many people we had grown to love and appreciate during our time at university.

After completing my House jobs in Southampton, I was advised by one of my consultants that it was now time to move away. In order to further my medical career I needed to gain experience in other places and he advised I should start applying for jobs in other parts of the country. This came as a great shock; both Sheelagh and I felt that Southampton was now our home. Surely God wanted us to continue to be part of the church. Telling my consultant of my decision to stay in Southampton prompted him to tell me that I was committing professional suicide, but this merely encouraged me to seek God to reaffirm his will for our lives.

Having decided at medical school that I would never do psychiatry or General Practice it was a surprise to me that in the latter part of my year as a Houseman I began to feel that God wanted me to look towards General Practice as a career. Initially, this thought did not excite me. However God continued to challenge me and I soon began to share his vision for a Christian Medical Practice where, hopefully, we could provide an excellent standard of medical care whilst looking at the needs of the whole person in terms of body, soul and spirit. To do this I would need to find a practice of like-minded people and this seemed highly unlikely. It was then that I met Barry Trewinnard, a Christian doctor who was working in Basingstoke. As we met and talked it became clear that Barry had a similar vision for General Practice. It would be no good, however, hoping to join an established practice: to fulfil our vision for the medical work, we would need to start a practice ourselves. (We later learned that this is rarely ever done, but in our youthful enthusiasm we believed we could do anything.)

Having settled in my mind that I would now stay in Southampton and pursue a career in General Practice I set about applying for jobs that would prepare me for this. If I were to do General Practice I decided that I wanted to have another skill within medicine that I could pursue alongside my practice work. The job that appealed to me was that of an anaesthetist. I approached the Anaesthetic Department in Southampton but was told there were no jobs currently available, but that they might consider me when the next post became vacant. Leaving the Chairman of the Department with my CV I felt confident that God would give me a job as soon as my House jobs were completed. As the end of my House year approached I became more than a little anxious. There had been no news from the Anaesthetic Department and I had no job to go to. Having just bought our first house this was a disaster. Sheelagh was nursing but her salary would scarcely cover our mortgage let alone our other expenses; with no other alternative, I signed on the dole.

This was a great challenge to my faith. Did God really want me to stay in Southampton? Did he really want me in General Practice? Was anaesthetics the thing that I should do? What was God saying? Was my previous consultant right, was I just committing professional suicide?

Through much prayer and through the encouragement of our friends we remained resolute to what we felt God had said. I set about doing up the house that we had just bought, trying to do things which required spending little or no money. The garden was a bit of a wilderness and I spent much of the summer clearing the garden and having bonfires almost every day. One warm September afternoon whilst wearing only an old pair of denim shorts and black with soot from the bonfire, I went inside to get a drink. The doorbell rang. Without giving thought to my appearance I answered the door and standing in front of me was the Chairman of the Anaesthetic Department offering me a job as an Senior House Officer in anaesthetics at Southampton General Hospital. Being on the dole for seven weeks had been a testing time but God had remained faithful.

So my training began in what was to become my
first love in medicine. I spent the next eighteen months
successfully passing my anaesthetic exams and facing the
constant temptation of a career as an anaesthetist. With
the prospect of being a consultant only four years after
starting anaesthetic training, it was a difficult temptation
to resist. The future looked bright but I always knew in
the back of my mind that God had given me a vision for
General Practice.

My anaesthetic induction involved six weeks of intensive training under the supervision of two wonderful
consultants. After six weeks I was slowly 'let loose' to
give anaesthetics to patients who required the least
complicated procedures. Although supervision was
always close at hand, I was allocated to day-surgical and
day-gynaecological lists, as the anaesthetic procedures
required for these lists were usually the simplest.

It was here for the first time in my medical career
that I was confronted with abortion. At the end of
every gynaecological day-list were two or three 'STOPs',
Suction Termination of Pregnancy, that required a
general anaesthetic. Initially, I gave this little thought.
Focusing all my concentration on getting the anaesthetic
right gave me little time to think what I was actually doing,
but as I became more relaxed in giving anaesthetics I
was forced to think about just what I was being asked to
do.

Having started at medical school in 1971 (following the
1967 Act of Parliament that allowed abortions for more
social reasons), this procedure had become common place
even before my training had started. However, in the five
years of training at medical school I cannot remember
ever talking about abortion either in our obstetric and
gynaecology lectures or in any lectures on ethics. (It may
have been that I had not been present at these lectures

although, barring the first term, I had generally shown good attendance.)

As a young anaesthetist, for the first time in my medical career, I was presented with the dilemma of abortion. As a Christian, what was I to do? What did God feel about abortion? Where does human life begin? Should I be involved in these procedures? These were questions that suddenly needed answers and to which I had given no thought at all.

As my training progressed I came to love the job more and more but at the same time I became more uncomfortable anaesthetising young women for abortions. I sought help from my peers in the church and we began to talk about some of these issues. To my shame now we rather lamely came to the conclusion that these abortions were going to happen anyway, and as I was 'only giving the anaesthetics' I could do very little to stop them happening. Fortunately, as time went on and my experience in anaesthetics grew, I was assigned to blocks of anaesthetic training within certain specialities such as cardiac anaesthetics, neurology, intensive care, etc. This had allowed me to avoid the day gynaecological lists and to live with my rather spineless response to abortion.

On reflection, this was perhaps the first time that I had really considered God's perspective of those who are helpless in society. What did God think? Who was that unborn child and how did God perceive him or her? What did he think of those mothers who were making such decisions and should I be thinking about what I thought about them too?

After almost eighteen months in anaesthetics the time had come to pursue the vision that God had given me. I applied for a General Practice training rotation lasting three years, which would take me through four hospital specialities, obstetrics and gynaecology, paediatrics, accident and emergency and general medicine with geriatrics. Each of these posts would be for six months and would be followed by a year of training in General Practice in Southampton. At that time, at the end of the 1970s, General Practice was proving to be a popular career choice for doctors, and for the two General Practice training posts in Southampton there were over seventy applicants. To my amazement I was short listed for the posts, along with Richard, a Christian friend of mine whom I had known from the year below me in medical school. For the two of us the job presented a new challenge. For the six months rotation through obstetrics and gynaecology we would be asked to do abortions. What was now a familiar uneasiness came back to haunt me. I knew that I had to say I couldn't be involved. What would happen if I was asked in my interview? Talking with my friend Richard about this, we both agreed if we were asked to do abortions the answer would be no.

The interview day arrived. As I walked into the room, I was overwhelmed by the vast array of faces that presented round the table: 12 doctors, consultants and GPs, as well as a hospital administrator. As the interview committee was so large each person only got to ask one question, so I thought the issue of abortion might not arise at all. I spotted the obstetrics and gynaecology consultant half way round the room. One by one the consultants asked their question and everything seemed to be going very smoothly up until the point where the obstetric consultant got to pose his question to me. 'Now Dr Clarke we are obliged to do a number of abortions in our department. Are you going to be happy to be involved in this procedure?' So this was it, yes or no. Without giving it a second thought I answered that, as a Christian, I could not be involved in the abortion procedure and I watched him scribble on the pad in front of him. I remember little more of the remaining five questions from the other consultants. I only remember thinking 'well, that's it; I am not going to get the job'. With only one question to ask it was obviously important to the gynaecology consultant that the successful candidate agreed to being involved in abortions. For Richard and me therefore, the chance of being appointed to the posts seemed to have slipped away.

The faithfulness of God is constantly astounding. Out of the huge number of applicants for the two General Practice training posts the two successful candidates were Richard and I, the two Christians who had both stated they would refuse to do abortions. Though I had lacked faith, God had remained faithful; the training posts in different departments were all hugely enjoyable.

My vision for providing General Practice grew and Barry Trewinnard and I began spending more time together discussing our ideas. Could it be that we could start a General Practice from scratch providing medicine with a holistic Christian approach? The medical establishment thought not. How could we survive financially? At that time you were paid in General Practice according to the number of patients on your list and for the services you provided to those patients. If you had no patients you got no money. How were we to get patients? Advertising was not allowed. Barry and I were now both married, we both had mortgages and Sheelagh and I had two young children. This was financial madness and yet our vision remained. We continued to pursue our dream.

Being a far better administrator and businessman than me, Barry approached the Family Practitioner Committee with our proposal and although they thought we were completely mad, they indicated there was an area of Southampton that was relatively under-doctored, and if we chose to do so we could quite legitimately set up a new General Practice in this area. The area was on the east side of Southampton and we began looking for premises that we might be able to afford to convert into a small General Practice. God led us to a small council estate nestled in the hills on the east side of the river, to a parade of derelict and rundown shops. Through Barry's powers of persuasion with a friendly bank manager we took over the lease of one of the shop units on the estate and converted it into a single surgery General Practice. We were enormously indebted to many members of our church who immediately signed on our list and gave us a basis of what is now a thriving General Practice. People in the estate passing the shop-front soon became curious as to what we had to offer and gradually we started to sign on new patients from the estate. We were helped considerably by our lovely receptionist, Grace, a church member who had previously worked in a hardware store on the parade. Because she was so well known local people felt comfortable coming into the surgery, having a chat, and finding themselves signing on to our list!

Over the course of three years our list size slowly grew to around one and a half thousand but this was far from what we needed to be a viable General Practice. Barry and I were both working in other jobs. Barry had started doing some work in orthopaedics and, to my delight, I had managed to secure a part-time post in anaesthetics. For one afternoon a week, I also worked in Accident and Emergency and I had just been invited into the eldership of the church. By doing all these jobs we were able to keep afloat financially, but only just. In the practice our overdraft was soon at its limit and the bank was unwilling to lend us any more. We needed a breakthrough and we desperately needed God's help.

Two and a half miles to the south of us, a practice in another socially deprived area of Southampton was in difficulties, so we began to pray about the possibility of taking it over completely. Through Barry's tenacity and much prayer we miraculously saw the resignation of the senior partner, which allowed us to successfully take over the entire patient list. Overnight we inherited another four and a half thousand patients and suddenly became a practice of over six thousand patients.

Since those early days we have grown to a practice of over eight thousand patients with two full-time partners and five part-time partners, all of whom are Christians. Two years ago I was able to reduce my hours to part-time but I continued to work in anaesthetics (which I have been able to do continuously for the past 22 years). As I have said earlier, the faithfulness of God is astounding. As I look back on my life, scraping into medical school, saying I would never stay in Southampton or go into General Practice, being told that I was foolish to stay in Southampton, God has worked miracle after miracle to bring Sheelagh and I together, placing on our hearts an altogether new passion.

The birth of the Firgrove Family Trust

In 1984 two significant events took place in the Community Church in Southampton. Firstly, at a leaders' training weekend three respected men in the church were invited to speak about 'evangelism'. Although they had no knowledge of the word each was to bring, there was one very clear central theme. The church should not simply talk about the good news of Jesus, but there should be a demonstration of God's love by reaching out to the broken hearted, the poor and the needy. At that time, the church had been faithful in preaching the gospel, but there had been no practical help to those who were in need.

The second event which was to have a dramatic effect on the direction of the church was an awkward question posed by Christine Thomas, the wife of one of our elders. Simply put, the question was: 'What do the elders feel is the Christian response to abortion?' During one of her pregnancies, Christine had read Tolkein's *Lord of the Rings* trilogy over the space of just a few days. She decided to do the same with the Bible. Reading right through the Bible over a three-month period, Christine was struck by the constant, recurring theme of God's compassion for those in need. Alongside this overwhelming extension of grace to the poor and needy, ran God's inherent hatred of injustice. Some time previously, Christine had received a communication from CARE (this is a well-established Christian charity that undertakes a variety of social caring and educational programmes as well as research and lobbying on associated issues) on the issue of abortion, but she had set it to one side. Reading the first chapter of Isaiah, Christine was challenged by verse 11:

> *When you spread out your hands in prayer, I will hide my eyes from you; even if you offer many prayers, I will not listen. Your hands are full of blood; wash and make yourselves clean.*

Picking up CARE's communication, Christine felt that God was speaking to her about the issue of abortion, and she began to feel God's grief at the loss of innocent life. Christine was not prepared to remain silent and responded by posing her question to the elders of the church.

This question echoed back to my early journey as a junior doctor, coming to the decision that in my jobs in gynaecology and anaesthetics, abortion was not something I wanted to be involved with. However, I had never really examined the issue of abortion much more deeply than this, but because of my professional training in medicine, the eldership team wanted me to formulate our response. Although in my own mind I knew I had already disagreed with abortion, a more detailed study of the scriptures revealed God's immense love for human kind and the unique value he places on every human life. I came to understand how abortion grieved the heart of God and that abortion was more than just the termination of an unwanted pregnancy. It involved a developing human life. We held a seminar in the church on the issue and together we began to seek God's heart.

The leadership conference and the challenge of Christine's question had now raised another question. If, as a church, we felt abortion was wrong, what were we going to do about it? With some friends from the church, we travelled to Phoenix, Arizona, where we met Dave and Joann Everitt, who were pioneering the establishment of Pregnancy Counselling Centres in the USA.

We returned home with a clear vision to set up a pregnancy crisis centre in Southampton, offering women a place of safety to come and talk about an unplanned pregnancy. We started up a steering committee and met every month, progressing slowly towards our goal. During the mid-1980s the pieces slowly fell into place. Firstly, we established a charitable trust under whose umbrella the centre would function. On setting up a new charitable trust we were advised not to use the names that were common among other Christian organisations and it was Adrian Thomas, Christine's husband, who suggested that we use the name Firgrove. This seemed a neutral-sounding name and was taken from the road name just along from our church building. The church raised £13,000 for the work and we decided to set aside £10,000 of this to put down as a deposit on a property. We wanted affordable premises near to a major bus route and easily accessible from all parts of town. God's faithfulness was amazing. The road from which we had taken our name, Firgrove Road, was a residential road but had one small business unit that was closing down. The old tailor shop was up for sale, its owner was retiring, and we were able to purchase the property at a very reasonable price, as it was not readily usable as a residential dwelling. This, of course, suited us perfectly as the building already had the correct business listing. So it was that the Firgrove Centre was established.

Alongside the establishing of the centre we set about educating the church across Southampton on the issue of abortion. We not only involved our own church members but sought the involvement of churches right across the city. (One of my chief joys in this work has been to see the involvement of Christians from many different churches.) From the congregations of the many supportive churches, people came forward to help on many different levels, giving financially, emotionally or practically, as well as offering to become involved as trained advisors or 'befrienders' at the centre.

It was during our first counsellor training that I met Joanna Thompson. In 1986 we knew of no other church-based pregnancy counselling centre in Great Britain. In an area as distressing and challenging as counselling crisis pregnancy, we wanted our counsellors to be trained professionally, but we were concerned about how to go about it. Generally the church had responded very poorly to the change of abortion laws in Great Britain, with the exception of the Catholic Church, which had always maintained a very clear response. However, a secular organisation called *Life* had pioneered the provision of pregnancy counselling centres to offer women with unplanned pregnancies an alternative to the abortion route. We found out that a group of women from one of the churches in Basingstoke were running the *Life* Centre there and it was to them that we turned for help with our counsellor training. They themselves had only been involved in the work for six months but this short experience was invaluable to us and we benefited enormously from their insights. Additional input from local social workers, counsellors, and from our own *Life* Centre in Southampton further helped us train our counsellors. In February 1987 the Firgrove Centre opened.

From the outset, the Firgrove Centre was established as a haven for women faced with the dilemma of an unexpected pregnancy. The core principle of Firgrove is to offer unconditional acceptance, non-judgemental and non-directive advice, and continual practical help. This ethic is borne out in the various emotional and practical needs of women that the centre seeks to meet.

Initially, pregnancy testing is offered freely and unreservedly to any woman. If she is found to be pregnant, the woman is then guided through the three options of keeping her baby, placing it for adoption, or having an abortion.

Women facing an unplanned pregnancy are confronted by numerous difficult situations. The centre aims to help the woman through her decision and ensure that she is not making a decision purely for financial or practical reasons which, with help, may be resolved. The centre therefore offers free baby clothes and baby equipment as well as advice and guidance on housing and benefits. Furthermore, the centre was able to establish two mother-and-baby homes for any homeless young women, set up as an interim solution whilst suitable council accommodation was sought. (Our two mother-and-baby homes have now closed, as the provision of this sort of accommodation has now been taken over by another Christian organisation.)

For other women facing an unplanned pregnancy, there is simply a need for friendship and support in order to see their pregnancy through. A team of 'befrienders' was established to provide this practical help and support. Facing an unplanned pregnancy as a single mother can be a daunting prospect. Having someone available to baby-sit existing children or perhaps provide meals, or even just be a listening ear, can sometimes make all the difference.

For women who choose the complex and at times painful decision of abortion, we also provide help and support, including post-abortion counselling, seeking to extend God's heart of love and compassion to women at a particularly traumatic time.

From those early days, the centre has grown and gone from strength to strength. We currently see between one and two thousand women a year and have seen as many as 20 in one day. We now own the centre premises, our annual budget is around £35,000 a year and we employ five women on a part-time basis. Alongside the work of the centre we have an education programme, going into schools and teaching on sex education and relationships, abortion and sexually transmitted infections. The need for such a programme grew from our desire to target the cause of unplanned pregnancies as well as the effects. The education programme is now very well respected part of the work and for many years we have been going into a large number of the senior schools in the Southampton area.

Encouraged by the success of the Firgrove Centre we set about extending the work countrywide. In May 1988 we had a conference in Southampton and sent invitations out around the country hoping that others would also come to share our vision. As well as the women from the church in Basingstoke we were aware of one or two other groups who had begun to provide crisis pregnancy counselling. We were staggered when around one hundred and fifty people attended the conference. Heartened by this response we continued to meet and work with the team from Basingstoke and this eventually led to the establishing of the organisation Christians Caring for Life (CCfL) in 1990. By that time, we knew of 27 pregnancy counselling centres that were being run by local churches and by the summer of 1992 this had grown to 43 centres. All these centres were independent and autonomous. We played no part in establishing centres; this was achieved by people independently responding to a God-given vision. CCfL merely sought to support, encourage, educate and provide resources for the growing work.

With an annual budget of only £2,000 it was becoming clear that we could not sustain the work of CCfL and in 1992 CARE provided advice and help. In June 1992 we held our first centre leaders' conference and the conference was addressed by Lyndon and Celia Bowring from CARE. Lyndon became part of the CCfL support team and with his help and encouragement our fledgling organisation was taken under CARE's wing to become CARE-for-Life. Joanna Thompson was taken on as our first national co-ordinator and CARE-for-Life soon became a thriving part of CARE's work.

There are now over 160 centres in all parts of the country and we have had the ongoing privilege of having input into centres right across the world. Particular links have been forged with centres in South Africa and Eastern Europe. CARE-for-Life has recently been renamed CARE Centres Network and the work continues to grow and flourish. We continue to seek to help women and families facing the dilemma of an unexpected pregnancy and to help women with post-abortion grief. Through the education work we are touching the lives of thousands of young people right across the country, and already there are encouraging signs that this work is having a dramatic effect. It has been impossible for me to recount in these few pages the miracles that God has worked to bring us to this place. In Philip and Joanna Thompson, Elaine Davies, Howard and Carol Chapman and the team in Basingstoke, the Care Centres Network support team, and the Firgrove Team from the many churches in Southampton, we have found true friendship.

In the introduction, I said that this book was not about abortion. It may seem strange therefore that I have set the context for the rest of the book around my early dealings with the issue of abortion. What I aim to show in the chapters that follow is that this story provides the context for my journey in understanding grace, which first manifested itself in the issue of abortion. I want to show that through God's work in pregnancy crisis centres, we can learn and understand his heart for all the broken and needy people in our society.

Two

Salt and Light

Let me tell you why you are here. You're here to be salt-seasoning that brings out God-flavors of this earth. If you lose your saltiness, how will people taste godliness? You have lost your usefulness and will end up in the garbage.

Here is another way to put it: You're here to be light, bringing out the God-colors in the world. God is not a secret to be kept. We're going public with this, as public as a city on a hill. If I make you light-bearers, you do not think I am going to hide you under a bucket, do you? I'm putting you on a light stand. Now that I've put you there on a hilltop, on a light stand – shine! Keep open house; be generous with your lives. By opening up to others, you will prompt people to open up with God, this generous Father in heaven.

Matthew 5:13–16, The Message

When I was a young boy growing up in Lincoln my parents were keen gardeners. Throughout the year, but particularly in the spring, my father would plant vegetables and through the late summer and autumn we would harvest them and then enjoy the fruit of his labours. One of the crops that grew particularly well was runner beans. In early autumn we had a bumper harvest and there were always far too many beans to eat at the time.

Having no freezer in those days, we preserved the beans by packing them down in layers of salt. I have vivid memories of helping my mother at the kitchen table, slicing the beans through a bean slicer and then packing handfuls of them between handfuls of salt in big jars. Throughout the long winter months we would bring the jars of beans out, wash the salt off them and enjoy them as if they had just been picked. On occasions we would find a jar where the beans had begun to go off. Now the question is, was it the fault of the beans that they went off, or was it that there was not enough salt?

In Matthew's gospel we have the account that we know now as the Sermon on the Mount. Jesus had taken his disciples, the fledgling church, up into the mountains where he taught them. He said to them 'You are the salt of the earth,' a challenge that their lives should be distinctive and healing, preserving the world from its moral decline. Today we face the same challenge. The world around us is morally decaying and the church of God should be the salt that helps to prevent this relentless decline. Just like the beans, whose fault is it if society decays? It has been well said: 'Evil prevails when good people do nothing.'

As well as being the 'salt of the earth' however, Jesus said 'You are the light of the world. Let your light so shine before men that they may see your good works and give glory to your Father who is in heaven.' This story resonated with me when, at the age of sixteen I went on a Crusader holiday to Clarens on the north-eastern shore of Lake Geneva, Switzerland. One of the planned day trips was to take the mountain railway from up behind the village to the top of the mountains, the Rochers de Naye, overlooking the lake. The day was warm and sunny and from the top of the mountain there were spectacular views. Having taken the easy route by train to the top, we decided that we would walk back down to the village. Although we were not equipped for mountain walking the paths and track down the mountain were easy and the weather was good. As we set off down the mountain in bright sunshine, we had no concerns. A mile or two from the summit we stood at the top of a long glacial valley and noticed that a few clouds had started rolling in. A gentle breeze was picking up.

The slight change in weather was of no concern and we stood at the top of the valley that stretched out for miles before us, towards the village. It was at that moment that we were faced with a very eerie sight. Looking like a great wave speeding up the valley towards us we realised, with some horror, that we were 'seeing' the wind, with all the trees and vegetation bowing before it. The wind was rushing towards us at a terrifying pace. Within seconds the skies darkened and seemed to go almost black. The breeze picked up. Suddenly it hit. A huge wall of wind that forced the trees to bend virtually horizontal; pine-cones rained all around us. I was literally blown off my feet and thrown across the track. The speed at which the events unfolded had left us little or no time to react.

Having been disorientated by the wind, the rain came and, with the skies now heavy with cloud, we searched for somewhere to shelter. The situation was becoming a little perilous and we felt that we shouldn't attempt our journey back to the village until the weather improved. In the midst of the storm, as we continued to search for the safety of shelter, two lights shone out in the gloom. Representing safety in the danger of the storm, we ran towards them and they led us to a barn, close to a mountain chalet. Once the worst of the storm had passed we slowly made our way back to the village, arriving very late and having caused much concern amongst the organisers of our party. We learned later that the train we would have caught down from the mountain had been blown off its tracks.

In this situation, the light we saw led us to shelter, shining out in the gloom and despair of the storm to show us the way to safety. If the church is to be 'the light of the world', we too should be the beacon of light that people run to when they seek comfort and shelter from the storms of life.

In the midst of our turbulent and troubled world do we stand out as beacons of light to whom people can run to in their hour of need? Do our good works shine out as beacons of hope to a hurting generation? Do people see the church as the answer to their desperate needs and come running towards the light to find a place of safety in the midst of their storm?

The opening story from Philip Yancey's incomparable book, *What's So Amazing About Grace?*, suggests that this is far from true. He relates this story, heard from a friend who worked in Chicago:

> *A prostitute came to see me in wretched straits, homeless, sick, unable to buy food for her two-year-old daughter. Through sobs and tears, she told me she had been renting out her daughter – two years old! – to men interested in kinky sex. She made more renting out her daughter for an hour than she could earn on her own in a night. She had to do it, she said, to support her own drug habit. I could hardly bear hearing her sordid story. For one thing, it made me legally liable – I'm required to report cases of child abuse. I had no idea what to say to this woman.*
>
> *At last, I asked if she had ever thought of going to church for help. I will never forget the look of pure, naïve shock that crossed her face. 'Church!' she cried. 'Why would I ever go there? I was already feeling terrible about myself. They'd just make me feel worse.'*[1]

Jesus said that we are to be the light of the world, and yet sadly, few people seem to consider the church as a place of hope when they are lost and broken. Is this because, instead of receiving unconditional acceptance and practical love, they find judgement and indifference? Walking along the high street yesterday, I saw a church notice-board proclaiming, 'God is love, Jesus proved it!', and I cringed: not because this statement is false, but as the followers of Jesus on earth today, *we* should prove it. The crowds flocked to Jesus as he went from town to town, yet today many of our churches lie empty, being sold off as coffee bars and night-clubs.

When I first became involved in the pregnancy counselling work, I read John Stott's excellent book *Issues Facing Christians Today* (now revised). I was immensely challenged by a poem written by a homeless woman and handed to a regional officer of Shelter. She had gone to a country vicar for help, and he (doubtless sincerely, and because he was busy and felt helpless) '… promised to pray for her'. The poem is a parody of the verses in Matthew 25:35–36.

I was hungry,
> And you formed a humanities group to discuss my hunger.

I was imprisoned,
> And you crept off quietly to your chapel and prayed for my release.

I was naked,
> And in your mind you debated the morality of my appearance.

I was sick,
> And you knelt and thanked God for your health.

I was homeless,
> And you preached to me of the spiritual shelter of the love of God.

I was lonely,
> And you left me alone to pray for me.

You seem so holy, so close to God,
> But I am still very hungry – and lonely – and cold.[2]

When I went to the United States, I returned having purchased a book by Larry Christenson. The book, *Social Action – Jesus Style* was written in the mid-1970s and begins:

> *We live in a day when critics inside and outside the church have raised the cry for Christian social action. 'What is the church doing about injustice, war, poverty, racism, ecology?' The question is rhetorical, not really a question at all. It is a critique: 'The church is not doing enough if, indeed, it is doing anything at all.'*[3]

Since Larry Christenson wrote these words, I believe the evangelical church has begun to respond to the challenge of social action, but there is still much, much more to do. Across Britain and worldwide, many churches are now becoming heavily involved with issues of social injustice, whilst at the same time reaching out to those whose lives are afflicted by those social injustices. Social action represents this two-fold work – tackling injustice and helping those in need.

The Prophet, Micah, denounces the corrupt life of Israel and Judah. Rich landowners were taking advantage of the poor (Mich. 2:1–2) and injustice was rife (2:6–11; 3:11) Through Micah, God reveals his anger at injustice and corruption and pronounces judgement on those who do such things. God then reminds his people (chapter 6) of the grace by which he chose them, and then what was required of them.

He has showed you O man what is good and what does the Lord require of you, to do justice and to love kindness and to walk humbly with your God.

Social action is not an option but an imperative for God's people. The social injustices of our day – poverty, racial hatred, war, corporate greed – and all the afflictions caused by social injustice – starvation, hunger, crime, family breakdown, alcoholism, drug abuse, etc. – require a response from the church. Giving a gift to Oxfam or Christian Aid or writing a cheque to Children in Need may appease our conscience, but it is not enough. The call to the church is, it is time to be involved.

Faced with the enormous needs of our society, it is easy to be overwhelmed and think 'What is the point? I can't make a difference.' When Mother Teresa was asked how she coped with the insurmountable need of the poor whom she served in Calcutta she replied, 'One by one.' When Christine Thomas raised her question to the elders of the church, challenging them on the issue of abortion, she could not have imagined that this one challenge would be used by God, leading to the establishing of not only a Crisis Pregnancy Centre in Southampton, but also a national organisation which is touching people in the UK and worldwide.

Oscar Romero, the Bishop of El Salvador, said this:

We cannot do everything. And there is a sense of liberation in realising that this enables us to do something and to do it very well. It may be incomplete but it is a beginning, a step along the way, an opportunity for the Lord's grace to enter and do the rest. We may never see the end results but that is the difference between the master builder and the worker. We are the workers not the master builders, we are the ministers not messiahs, we are the prophets of a future not our own.[4]

Social action has only been a recent priority for many churches. In the history of the church however, this has not always been the case. One of the greatest examples of a Christian being involved in social action is that of Anthony Ashley-Cooper, seventh Earl of Shaftesbury, who lived in the nineteenth century. Born on the 28th April 1801 into an aristocratic family, his childhood was severe and devoid of the security of parental love. He had one friend, however, a housekeeper, Anna Maria Milles. Each evening before bed, Maria would sit with young Anthony, reading him stories from the gospels; she also began to teach him how to pray. This input from Maria clearly had a profound effect on Anthony and even from such a tender age it was evident that he had a real and personal faith. At the age of ten, away at school, Anthony learned that Maria had died. Despite being taunted by his school friends, Anthony drew on Maria's teachings and turned to God, finding comfort in his faith through reading the Bible and praying.

Soon after this, Anthony's uncle, the fifth Earl of Shaftesbury, died aged forty-nine. Anthony's father promptly succeeded as the sixth Earl of Shaftesbury and his son, Anthony, took on the title of Lord Ashley. It was at the age of sixteen that an incident occurred which was to have a profound effect on Lord Ashley's life.

He was walking alone down Harrow Hill when he heard shouting and yelling, and then drunken singing. He stopped. To his disgust he saw four or five tipsy men lurching up a side street under the weight of a rough coffin, the kind used only for paupers. As they turned the corner on their way to the church yard one of them stumbled and the coffin fell to the ground. The men let out a stream of oaths.

Ashley felt sick. a fellow human being was to be buried with no mourners, his remains degraded by the drunken antics of men who cared nothing. 'Good heavens!' thought Ashley.

'Can this be permitted simply because the man was poor and friendless?'[5]

So began the amazing life of a man who chose to become involved. In her biography of Shaftesbury, Georgina Battiscombe wrote, 'No man has in fact ever done more to lessen the extent of human misery, or to add to the sum total of human happiness.'[6]

At the age of twenty-five he entered Parliament as an MP in the House of Commons. He immediately set the course for his parliamentary career by enquiring into the treatment of 'lunatics' – those who were mentally ill. By visiting the establishments where these people were held he saw first-hand the appalling conditions of cruelty and inhumanity that were so prevalent in his day.

Having tackled one social injustice he turned his efforts to the conditions under which children worked in factories, mills and mines, to the climbing boys or chimney-sweeps and to the plight of children in the slums of London. As if this were not enough Lord Ashley was also involved in the establishing of the Church Pastoral Aid Society 'for increasing the number of working clergymen in the Church of England, and encouraging the appointment of pious and discreet laymen as helpers to the clergy and duties not ministerial.' This he did because of his 'heartfelt and earnest desire to see the Church of England, the church of the nation and especially of the very poorest classes, that she might dive into the recesses of human misery and bring out the wretched and ignorant sufferers to bask in the light and life and liberty of the gospel.' His passion for the Christian gospel was boundless. He was President of the Bible Society and a supporter of the London City Mission, Young Man's Christian Association and the Church Missionary Society.

When his father died aged fifty, Lord Ashley inherited the title and became the seventh Earl of Shaftesbury. Lord Longford once wrote, 'In the history of social reform in England, no name compares with Shaftesbury.'[7] Indeed, his name and his legacy live on now in the Shaftesbury Society which describes itself as 'a national Christian charity working for inclusion, empowerment and justice as well as providing education and residential services for disabled people. Shaftesbury works with churches in urban areas affected by depravation, helping them to respond in practical and relevant ways to community needs.'

If we are ever tempted to ask ourselves again 'What can I do? Where do I begin?' we need only look at the lives of these people. By simply getting involved – however insignificant your contribution may seem – you can make a huge difference. The radical changes in social justice seen in this country throughout the eighteenth and nineteenth centuries accompanied the evangelical revival within the church. John Wesley's preaching not only led people to Christ but also inspired a new social conscience. A new generation of evangelical leaders who followed Wesley at the end of the eighteenth century, were centred on Clapham in south London and became known as the Clapham Sect.[8] Under the leadership of William Wilberforce they brought abolition to the slave trade, to slave smuggling and finally the granting of slaves their freedom.

The torch of social action was kept aflame by Shaftesbury and he ensured that the fire burned strongly in the next generation. At a tea party in March 1872, Shaftesbury encouraged other mission leaders to reach out further in the realms of social action. Among those present was a young Thomas Barnardo 'who gave a graphic account of discovering destitute children on the rooftops.'[9] Also present at their tea party was Catherine Booth who was standing in for her husband, William Booth, who six years later renamed his Christian mission the Salvation Army. The organisations that these men birthed remain with us today, gracing our world with kindness and practical Christian love. With such a heritage it is hard to understand why the modern church has failed to take on the baton of social action.

John Stott chronicles the reasons for the 'great reversal'.[10] This reference outlines the decline in social involvement by the church and attributes this decline to a number of reasons.

From my observation of the Christian church at large I see there to be two main reasons for a lack of involvement in social action. Firstly, there seems to be a great fear that we will somehow 'water down' the gospel, if we allow ourselves to get entangled in social action. This fear was voiced at the beginning of the twentieth century, when it was felt that social action detracted from the fundamental preaching of the gospel, and churches began to step back. There is certainly a danger that our involvement in social action can become the overriding influence in our life, to the point where our individual commitment to Christ and our day-to-day walk with him can be affected. We have constantly stressed in our work with the Firgrove Centre and with Care Centres Network that the issue of abortion is not our 'cause'. We are not fighting for an issue. Our passion is for Jesus; knowing him, and living by the daily bread of his word (Mt. 4:4). If we allow our involvement to be a substitute for our relationship with Christ then there is a danger that we will lapse into legalism and what Larry Christenson calls Pharisaism and against which danger he warns:

> … *It slips in unannounced. It mingles among people who have experienced an outpouring of spiritual life. It bandies about religious terminology with glib facility. Its zeal and*

*earnestness gain attention and accommodation, it fastens upon
the readiness for dedication in the newly awakened. Its objectives
are so praiseworthy, and its goals so unimpeachable, that the
exhortations can scarcely be gainsaid. 'You want to be truly
holy don't you? If you are really a Christian, surely you will
join supporting this ...' Subtly the focus shifts from what God
does to what man must do.*[11]

In many ways, the Christian walk is down a very narrow
path (Mt. 7:14) and yet this pathway is the pathway of
freedom, liberty and joy. It is the pathway of abiding in
Christ. On the one side are the dangers of legalism and
Pharisaism, on the other side the dangers of liberalism and
licence. The way the Bible describes it is like this:

*And an highway shall be there, and a way, and it shall be called
The way of holiness; the unclean shall not pass over it; but it
shall be for those: the wayfaring men, though fools, shall not
err therein. No lion shall be there, nor any ravenous beast shall
go thereon, it shall not be found there; but the redeemed shall
walk there. (Is. 35:8–9, Authorized Version).*

The path that God has provided for us, the way of holiness,
is the daily walk of a living relationship with Jesus. Each
day we are called to live by the 'bread' of his word, not
relying on legalistic rules and formulas or things that
worked for us yesterday, nor allowing the gracious
freedom of our walk to be an excuse for slipping into
behaviour beyond the framework of God's plans for us.
This daily journey is the pathway of grace and truth and
one to which we will return in chapter 6.

The second reason why we have seen a decline in
social involvement within the modern church is, I believe,
because of the immense cost that is incurred if we truly
get involved. As people within God's church we have

allowed ourselves to be influenced by the values of the world and the ways of modern society, and have failed to count the true cost of commitment to God. As I write this I realise that I am guilty of this myself; it is so much easier to put some money in the plate for an offering for the poor than to roll up our sleeves and get involved with people directly.

In Southampton, Bob and Colette Light have set an amazing example to us, through the 'Flower of Justice' project. Bob, an ex-drug addict was brought up on one of the estates in Southampton. He and Colette have now returned to live and work there, bringing hope to hundreds of people. Running children's clubs, organising weeks of fun events during school holidays, offering debt counselling, and providing for the needs of the poor, their commitment is twenty-four hours of every day. As time has gone on, this physical commitment has touched the lives of a significant number of people on the estate and already many have made commitments to God and joined the church. If we are prepared be get involved, we will see the results of God's work.

Bob's Story

Bob was born in the Woolston area of Southampton in May 1951. His parents were caring and always provided for the family, but they were never able to demonstrate their love emotionally. This emotional poverty was common to their generation. In his early teens, despite having natural ability, he began to lose confidence at school and started hanging out with a friend who introduced him to smoking cannabis and sniffing solvents.

Bit by bit, Bob lost sight of his schooling and his future; drugs became his whole life. Doing a paper round to earn some money he was able to satisfy his drug habit by buying fifty pence worth of cannabis a week on a Friday night.

One Friday, Bob arrived to find his dealer had run out of his usual supply. Undeterred, Bob turned to another dealer who immediately befriended him and took him to the park to smoke cannabis. This was simply a ploy to introduce Bob to heroin, which the dealer eventually offered to Bob as they sat smoking. To begin with Bob refused, as he hated needles, and was not prepared to inject himself. However, the dealer persisted, and said that he would inject Bob the first time and everything would be all right. With just one shot Bob was hooked. The heroin shut his world out. Nothing could touch him now.

Sinking deeper into the drug culture Bob was soon being supplied with drugs direct from his GP. At the age of seventeen he was admitted to a psychiatric hospital for his first detoxification. At the end of the sixties this comprised of being tied to the bed and left alone, filled with of tranquilliser and given electric shock treatment (normally reserved for the severely depressed). After three weeks of this so-called 'detox' Bob was discharged, but in his interview with the psychiatrist before leaving he said that he would probably return to taking drugs and incredibly his psychiatrist gave him a prescription for heroin.

By the time of his first marriage at the age of twenty-six, he had been 'sectioned' into psychiatric hospital five times from mental symptoms associated with drug use, and for detox. His new wife was also a drug addict and together they would get prescriptions for methadone from their GP, selling some of it to make money. For Bob this was not enough and he decided that in order to really make enough money to feed his habit he would need to become a big-time dealer. He went to Chinatown in London and made contact with one of the city's drug barons. This led him to become the biggest supplier of heroin in Southampton and he soon found himself in trouble with the police.

A short spell in prison was followed by six years on probation during which time Bob studied agriculture. He eventually moved to Cornwall and took a job as a farm hand. However, it was clear that Bob was still addicted to drugs and his marriage soon fell apart. Being thrown out of his family home, Bob soon became mentally ill and he was treated by the local psychiatrist. Rather than encouraging him to get clean, he was told 'Just accept it Bob, you are an addict, you always will be. You have just got to acknowledge that you will die a junkie.'

Even though deep down Bob really wanted to change, the input he was receiving from his psychiatrist led him to believe that this would be impossible. Sinking further into despair and depression he persuaded the chemist to give him a three-day supply of drugs, saying that he was going to Scotland and would not be able to come for his daily collection. He drove himself up onto the moors and injected the three-day supply all at once, hoping not to wake up.

A knock on the car window the following morning made him jump. He wound down the window and was confronted by a man asking if he was all right. In the darkness the evening before, Bob hadn't noticed that he had pulled into a lay-by outside a cottage, and the man at the window took him in. The man was an evangelist from the local church and offered Bob accommodation in his caravan across the road. As Bob was still living rough, he was very pleased to accept.

Each day the evangelist spent an hour with Bob talking to him about Jesus and taking him along to a church on Sundays. Unlike the people of the local town, the church congregation did not recoil from Bob. They would often just come and give him a hug or put their arm around him and gradually Bob began to find love and acceptance. Bob could not get over their kindness. Longing to get free from his drugs habit, he asked Jesus to change his life. In the same week the church prayed for him to stop smoking cigarettes and then had a two hour prayer time for healing from his drugs addiction. During this time God miraculously touched Bob's life and freed him from drugs. Bob threw away all the drugs, syringes and needles that he had in his pocket. Since that time has never taken drugs of any kind.

When his psychiatrist found out that he was no longer taking his drugs, he rang him urgently to offer to take Bob along to the chemist to get a supply, because she was so convinced that stopping his drugs so precipitously would cause him great harm. Bob was able to testify to God's goodness and declined her offer.

During this time Bob had got to know two other drug addicts, Doug and Teresa, who lived together. Quite independently of Bob's encounter with God, they also became Christians and their miraculous transformation made local headline news – JESUS SETS FREE THREE JUNKIES.

Eight years ago, Bob returned to Southampton and moved in with his mother, in the Swaythling area of town. Wanting to find a church he opened *Yellow Pages* and was drawn to the advert for Community Church. Attending the next Sunday morning Bob knew immediately that this was the place God wanted him. Bob soon developed a heart of compassion for the people on his estate. With a friend from the Swaythling area, he started to walk around the estate, praying. Through these walks Bob's vision grew and he knew then that he needed to commit to the area long-term. An opportunity arose on the estate and Bob was able to move in to a house there with his new wife, Colette, who had also recently become a Christian.

Bob started doing voluntary work in different schools, educating young people about drugs and he also worked in local prisons. Not earning very much, and living largely off social security benefits, Bob knew that he wanted to secure a better job. When Colette noticed an advert in the local paper for a project worker in a hostel, she encouraged Bob to apply. Bob felt this was a waste of time as he knew at interview he could not lie about his past, but he went along nevertheless and told the interviewers his story. He did not go straight home that day, but by the time he did the hostel had been on the phone three times to offer him the job! He did this job for five and a half years and progressed to become senior project worker.

During these years Bob and Colette started work on the Swaythling estate and opened Club Zion, a club for young people. To begin with very few children came but slowly the club grew and then parents began to come along to find out what was happening at the club, 'because their children were going home and behaving themselves.' Involvement with the lives of people on the estate meant that life for Bob and Colette was becoming very hectic. Bob would come back from his project work at the hostel worn out and he knew something had to give. It was then that three city businesses offered to pay a salary for him to work as a community project worker on the estate. Southampton Community Church also became involved, as did the Shaftesbury Society, who are currently working alongside Bob and Colette.

Bob and Colette are not simply involved in social action, they are living it. Working in their community they simply provide for the needs of their neighbours: reading letters for the blind elderly people; doing the gardens for the pensioners and disabled; running a kids club; looking out for the lonely and providing help where a need arises. Each year they run a community week, aimed at providing fun for whole families with barbecues, games and friendship. Last year over three hundred people attended every day. Families who were at war with each other are now getting on and as Bob said 'even the drug dealers supported it and gave us money.'

Many estate families are in debt to the tune of thousands of pounds. Through his work on the estate Bob has been able to provide food for these families while they use their own meagre resources to slowly pay off their debts. By feeding a family for several months, they were able to see their debt reduce from £5,000 to £500 and they are now independent again.

When I interviewed Bob and he related his story he said 'I used to think I was a nobody, that I was useless, and couldn't do anything. God has changed me and given me back my self respect, my self image.' Through his work in the 'Flower of Justice' project Bob is seeing God work similar miracles in the lives of hundreds of people, giving them back their sense of worth and value, and transforming their lives.

I reiterate that fundamental evangelicals have often criticised social involvement saying that it detracts from 'preaching the gospel': the Gospel of salvation through faith in Christ is the very foundation of our Christian life. As a teenager in Lincoln, I recognised my sinfulness before God and recognised that I was lost and separated from my Heavenly Father. Accepting Christ into my life, in a simple act of faith, rescued me from my hopelessness. I embarked upon a relationship with God and because I have found this journey to be so good I have always tried to tell other people about it. I have often done this in General Practice, though obviously, I have to recognise that I am not there for this reason and that I should not abuse my position. However, faced with seemingly hopeless situations and very little to offer either medically or socially I have sought people's permission to convey my faith and the exciting life that I discovered so long ago. I have to say that to date there has been seemingly little fruit in my efforts at 'preaching the gospel'. Our medical practice has, however, been instrumental in the lives of many people finding faith in Jesus Christ. By trying to live our faith in a practical way, meeting people at their point of need, we have been more successful in conveying the good news of Jesus than by preaching a gospel of words they don't understand, and can't relate to.

Working into socially deprived areas, simply conveying the words of the gospel may not be sufficient to persuade people there is a better way of living. People find it hard to believe that Jesus loves them when their alcoholic husband comes back in the evening and beats them up, or when they are so hard up they don't know where the next meal is coming from. People don't know there is a caring God when they are agoraphobic and cannot even leave their house.

In the early years of our General Practice a young agoraphobic mother had been referred to our practice counsellor for help with her mental illness. As it was coming up to Christmas, her main concern was that she was unable to go out and buy presents for her children, and the distress that this was causing her was deepening her mental torment. It may seem strange that something as simple as Christmas shopping could cause such distress, but to an agoraphobic this can seem like a mountain that is insurmountable. Faced with this dilemma, our practice counsellor, Brenda Henderson (who is a Christian), offered to go with her to do her Christmas shopping and be with her all the time in case she started to panic. Brenda took her into Southampton, helped her do her shopping and sat and had coffee with her in a coffee bar (Brenda admitted to feeling guilty doing this in 'work time'). The young mother could not get over the kindness and love that was shown to her, nor could she believe that she had been able to climb this mountain herself. Through Brenda's love and ongoing commitment this young woman not only bought her Christmas presents, but found new life in Jesus.

Brenda need not have felt guilty for taking time out to drink coffee. Although we employed her in the practice as a counsellor, a job for which she was exceedingly well trained, our heart was (and still is) to simply meet the needs of people in the most appropriate way. Brenda used to visit an elderly lady every week, 'just for a chat', and yet each week this old lady sat with tears streaming down her face, not able to believe that someone could be bothered with her. Brenda was able to bring her comfort in her loneliness, and hope and a sense of value. Another elderly lady aged eighty-two, had lived in Southampton all of her life, and yet had never once been outside the city boundary. Brenda was able to drive her the few miles to the New Forest and had the joy of experiencing the wonder in her eyes as she saw the forest for the very first time. Brenda did not 'preach the gospel', she didn't have to. She simply loved each person, meeting them at their point of need, but through her kindness she would often have the opportunity to speak naturally about her faith.

About twenty years ago, when we visited Dave and JoAnn Everitt in Phoenix, Arizona, their church had fairly recently had an 'evangelistic crusade'. Through the efforts of 'preaching the gospel' one person had been added to the church. At the same time, through Dave and JoAnn's work in the crisis pregnancy centre, twenty-six people had found faith in Christ. In a recent communication I had with Dave, he says, 'Pregnancy Resource Centres [their new name] are more successful in providing opportunities for sharing "the Gospel" than many churches.'

In February a few years ago I went with my daughter, Catherine, to New York to work with the church community of Pastor Diane Dunne, at Hope for the Future Ministries. Pastor Diane had received a vision from God to feed the poor and hungry on the streets of New York and, from humble beginnings, she had faithfully done this. In simple obedience to God, Diane grew her ministry from providing a few sandwiches to one or two people, to feeding hundreds of people week by week, providing them with nourishment and clothes, and providing them with hope. From among these poor, on the streets of New York, she now has a thriving church.

I do not want you to feel that I am negating the power of the spoken Gospel of Christ. Far from it! I came to salvation through the spoken Word powerfully preached. However, we need to get a balance in our evangelistic zeal and convey God's love by combining the preaching of the spoken word with acts of mercy and kindness, and demonstrations of God's miraculous power. There is no doubt that we need to 'preach the gospel', but our involvement in social action allows us to build a platform from which to speak. What right have I to speak on abortion, unless I am prepared to help women facing a crisis pregnancy? As we get involved in the lives of hurting people, the love of God begins to be revealed to them, allowing their hearts to hear the tender calling of a loving Father.

Milo and Jo's Story

Colette first met Jo through Club Zion, the kids club she and Bob had started on the estate. Jo was a parent, coming to see what her children were getting into, and wondering why they were returning home so different. Colette befriended Jo and Jo introduced her to her husband, Milo, who had alcohol and drug problems, and was in trouble with the police. Milo was brought before the court on burglary charges and, because of his previous record, was likely to receive a lengthy prison sentence. With Milo facing this daunting prospect, Bob went with him and was able to speak up for him in court. Bob promised the judge that he would help Milo with his difficulties at home, but nevertheless Milo was handed a two-and-a-half year jail sentence which was to be spent at Ford Open Prison. Although Bob felt somewhat discouraged by the sentence, Milo's barrister reassured him that with Milo's record, he had been let off very leniently indeed.

With Milo in prison, Jo became very depressed. The house and garden soon became extremely untidy, but Bob and Colette organised garden clearing and cleaning up the house along with other practical help to help Jo through. Alongside this they would take Jo to visit Milo in prison. They also started praying for Milo and Jo as a couple. Shortly after this Jo began to come out of her depression and one day announced that she had stopped her anti-depressant tablets. Quite suddenly, it seemed to Bob and Colette, she had become a different person. Bob and Colette had not pushed the gospel; they had simply loved Jo and had provided practical help in a time of need. A while later Jo came to Colette saying that she wanted to give her life to God.

On the same day that Jo became a Christian, unbeknown to her, Milo gave his life to God following an Alpha course in prison. With Milo now out of prison, Jo and Milo work together within the 'Flower of Justice' project helping others in the same way that they were once helped themselves.

Ghandi once said: 'If Christians lived according to their faith, there would be no more Hindus left in India' (source unknown). At the beginning of this new century I believe God is calling us again to live out the fullness of our faith, to count the cost, to be involved, and to really become the Salt and Light to our generation.

3

And Who Is My Neighbour?

*And behold, a lawyer stood up to put Him to the test,
saying, 'Teacher what shall I do to inherit eternal life?'
He said to him, 'What is written in the law. How do you
read?' And he answered, 'You shall love the Lord your God
with all your heart, and with all your soul, and with all
your strength, and with all your mind; and your neighbour
as yourself.' And (Jesus) said to him, 'You have answered
right; do this, and you will live.'*

*But (the lawyer), desiring to justify himself, said
to Jesus, 'And who is my neighbour?' Jesus replied, 'A
man was going down from Jerusalem to Jericho, and
he fell among robbers, who stripped him and beat him,
and departed, leaving him half dead. Now by chance a
priest was going down the road; and when he saw him,
passed by on the other side. So likewise a Levite, when
he came to the place and saw him, passed by on the
other side. But a Samaritan, as he journeyed, came to
where he was; and when he saw him, he had compassion,
and he went to him and bound up his wounds, pouring
on oil and wine; then he set him on his own beast and
brought him to an inn, and took care of him. And the
next day he took out two dinarii and gave them to the
innkeeper, saying, "Take care of him; and whatever
more you spend, I will repay when I come back." Which
of these three, do you think, proved a neighbour to the
man who fell among the robbers?' He said, 'The one who*

*showed mercy on him.' And Jesus said to him, 'Go and
do likewise.'*

Luke 10:25–37

Looking at the parables of Jesus, it is useful to try and
understand a bit of the context of these stories. I have been
helped immensely by reading the works of Kenneth Bailey,
who has lived and worked in the Middle East for many
years. His books, *Poet and Peasant* and *Through Peasant
Eyes* give a fascinating insight into the life of the peasant
and farming community in the Middle East at the time
of Christ, and his understanding of Jewish and Eastern
culture helps us comprehend these parables more fully.

Jerusalem was set up on the mountain heights of Judea
and a winding road of about twenty-five kilometres
descended the mount to Jericho, on the plains just west of
the River Jordan. The road was dangerous, meandering
through known bandit country. Throughout history, this
road has always been dangerous; in the Middle Ages a
fort was even built, halfway along the route. The heights
of Jerusalem afforded cooler days in the summer but
during the winter months Jericho offered a more hospitable
climate. Herod built his winter palace there and Jericho
became a fashionable resort for wealthy Jews and possibly
provided a place of retreat for the Jewish priests. It was in
Jericho that Zaccheus, the very rich tax collector, was met
by Jesus. The priests, who lived in Jericho, would ascend
the road to Jerusalem to perform their priestly duties in the
Temple, which would have included ritual purification.

Coming back down the road, a priest and Levite, ritually
clean from their temple duties, would not have welcomed
the sight of an 'unclean' man. In the Middle East, a person's
status and creed would have been obvious by the clothes
that they were wearing, or certainly by their speech. But
here was a man who was stripped of his clothes and left

for dead. He was unconscious, and was therefore unable to speak. The travellers down the road would not have known who he was or whether he was even a Jew. If the priest or Levite attended to him, would they become ritually unclean?

Between the orthodox Jews in Jerusalem and the south of Judea, and the unorthodox 'sect' of the Samaritans in the north, a rift had arisen. The history of this seems a little uncertain and the only reference to Samaritans in the Old Testament (2 Kgs. 17:29) suggests a pagan influence in their worship. The mix of pagan and Jewish rites were at odds with each other. In the New Testament when Jesus first sends out his disciples with the message of good news, he specifically asks them not to go to the towns of the Samaritans but first to go to the lost sheep of the house of Israel (Mt. 10:5). Furthermore, in Luke 17:6, we see Jesus, having healed ten lepers, calls the one Samaritan leper who came back to thank him a 'foreigner'.

These words of Jesus should in no way lead us to believe that he lacked compassion for the Samaritan people. Jesus displays his full heart of love and compassion for all men. Not only did he heal the Samaritan leper, but he chose a Samaritan woman to display his divine nature (Jn. 4:9). And it was not just this Samaritan woman who came to faith. The passage in John tells us that many others in her village also believed. Although Jesus commanded his disciples not to go to the villages of the Samaritans on their early mission, we see in Acts that these very same disciples took their preaching to 'many villages of the Samaritans' (8:25).

It was in this context that Jesus brought the parable that we now know as the Parable of the Good Samaritan. A Jewish lawyer had come to him to try to test him and asked the question which has burned on the heart of many throughout the centuries: 'Teacher, what must I do to inherit eternal life?' Responding to his orthodox questioner Jesus refers straight back to the Jewish law and yet, in doing so, he emphasises the fundamental basis of our Christian faith. Our eternal salvation is based on an ever-growing relationship of love and devotion to God through Jesus Christ, and an expression of that relationship through our love for one another. These two tenets of our faith can never be divorced.

Not wishing to lose face, the lawyer tries to justify himself by asking Jesus another question, 'And who is my neighbour?' It is then Jesus tells this remarkable parable which the religious leader must have found difficult to swallow. Jesus sets the scene of a man on a journey down a winding road through bandit country. He is suddenly set upon and left for dead. Faced with the needs of this hurting, dying man, Jesus challenges the inactivity of the religious community and chooses a despised Samaritan to convey the heart of love which Jesus demands of his disciples. In responding to the lawyer, Jesus does not answer the question, 'Who is my neighbour?' But instead, by revealing attitudes of the heart, he returns with a question to the lawyer, asking 'Who had actively behaved as a neighbour?' The lawyer could not even bring himself to say the word 'Samaritan', but responded, 'The one who showed mercy upon him.'

There is no doubt that we have been created by a God of love who desires that each one of us, through a living relationship with him, should outwork and display his heart of love to those around us. I personally find that living out this teaching is a constant and daily challenge. We face a spiritual battle with the mind-set of this age. Modern society has become self-centred, the 'me society' where egocentrism reigns. Speaking to a gathering of priests a couple of years ago, Cardinal Cormac Murphy-O'Connor, the Catholic Archbishop of Westminster said

People are seeking transient happiness in alcohol, drugs, pornography and recreational sex. There is indifference to Christian values in the church among many young people and, indeed, not only the young. You see quite a demoralised society, one where the only good is what I want, the only rights are my own and the only life with any meaning or value is a life that I want for myself ... When we live in a culture which says, what I have got is what I am, we are in big trouble. [1]

Recently, I watched a programme on television identifying the enormous level of financial debt amongst many people in our country today. The programme revealed people who, excluding their house mortgage, were in debt to the tune of £40,000 all of which was accumulated on credit cards on which they had purchased more and more to feed their extravagant lifestyles. The consumerism and value society places on material things seem to know no bounds. If we are to outwork our Christian faith along the lines that Jesus reveals through this parable, we need to rediscover the unrivalled promises we find in God, and as God's church become true salt and light giving a distinctive flavour and providing a shining example in a crumbling society.

The self-orientation of our current society has not led to greater happiness; rather, it has produced exactly the opposite. A computer software system that we used until recently in our General Practice was able to rank my patient diagnoses into the conditions that I most commonly saw. By far and away the most common problem that I face in General Practice is that of depression, and I may see as many as five patients with depression in any one surgery. The simple diagnosis masks the human tragedy of so many human lives. The journey from Jerusalem to Jericho as told by Jesus reflects the day-by-day journey of each one of our lives. Along the road we will meet those whose lives have been battered and broken by the 'thief', identified as Satan by Jesus, in John 10:10, and my daily challenge is to be the Samaritan and not the priest.

The priest, the Levite and the Samaritan were all confronted with an identical scene: a wretched, dirty man left for dead. It was their response to this scene which differentiated them and their response was guided by a simple choice. Two of them chose indifference and inactivity but 'the one who showed mercy', chose to interrupt his own journey to turn aside and help. It is surprising how often this simple choice presents itself. It is not always the choice of being involved in major ministry, but in the simple choice of helping somebody who appears to be in need.

During my trip to New York to work with Pastor Diane Dunne at the Hope for the Future Ministries, I was privileged to meet a young lady called Jenny who was from a church in South London. Jenny had captured God's heart for the poor and was fearless in her approach to helping people. During the time we were in New York we had a day off and spent time viewing the sights of the downtown area. On the subway back home a young woman boarded the train whose face was covered in blood having apparently been beaten. The rest of the commuters on the train assumed complete indifference and inactivity, but for Jenny this was not the right response. Without giving it another thought she went over to the young woman, offered her help and sat with her during her journey home. Whilst caring for this young woman in a very practical way, Jenny was also able to convey to her God's love. All around us in today's society there are people who are hurting. We do not need to go and seek them out: the challenge is simply not to 'pass by on the other side'.

The thing that I find most difficult about the parable of the Good Samaritan is the cost that Jesus demands from me. Jesus said: 'If a man would come after me, let him deny himself and take up his cross and follow me. For whoever would save his life will lose it and whoever loses his life for my sake will find it' (Mt. 16:24). Making the choice to halt our journey, to help those who are in need is a costly one. First of all, it may be inconvenient. There was a suggestion that Jericho was the country retreat for the religious fraternity and it is possible that Jesus was alluding to the fact that these religious men were taking time out in recreation, relaxation and leisure. How inconvenient and sacrificial, therefore, would it be to stop and help a broken man? The choice for the Samaritan was inconvenient too, and it took him out of his way to find a place of sanctuary. This cost him his time (that commodity seemingly so precious in our modern society) but having decided to give up his time he then gave up his possessions, his oil and wine. Next he gave up his comforts by setting the man on his own donkey to bring him to the inn. After all of this he gave his money. Furthermore, he pledged an ongoing commitment in time and money by saying, 'Whatever more you spend I will repay you *when I come back*' (my emphasis). The price that Jesus demands is our time, our possessions, our comforts, our money, and our ongoing commitment: simply put, it costs us everything.

Roger and Carol's Story

When I was working in General Practice full time, not only were the hours long, but the demands of the job were very stressful. From starting at 7.30 on a Monday morning I would often work through to Wednesday night by which time I would already have worked thirty-six hours and would be desperately looking forward to a half day on Thursday. Coming home from work on a Wednesday evening, I would often go straight to bed, much to the despair of Sheelagh and the family. And so it was that when Carol walked through the door in my Wednesday evening surgery, my only thoughts were to get through my work, get back home, have a large glass of red wine and get to bed.

From the moment I saw Carol I knew things were not good. Earlier that week I had admitted Carol's husband, Roger, into hospital, with some very bizarre symptoms suggestive of a rare and serious brain infection. I had known Roger, Carol and their two children for many years and, in fact, they had attended some church meetings and shown some interest in a faith in Christ, although neither of them at that time had made any commitment to God. Sitting down beside my desk and in obvious distress, Carol began to relate to me that Roger had a confirmed diagnosis of encephalitis. Following his admission, his condition had deteriorated rapidly and he had been transferred from the medical ward to the high care ward where he had continued to go down hill. He had then started to have continuous epileptic seizures and was again transferred to the intensive care unit at the Neurological Centre where he was put on life support systems. His doctors had prepared Carol for the worst: they were not expecting Roger to survive. If he were to survive there would be a strong possibility of permanent neurological damage.

After relating the severity of Roger's medical condition Carol suddenly said, 'Dr Clarke will you come and pray for him? If you come and pray for him he will get better.' To my shame I have to confess my first thought was 'Oh no!' Firstly, I was completely exhausted and the last thing on earth I wanted to do was to go from the surgery up to the hospital to pray for somebody. Secondly, my faith was not in line with Carol's: my medical training was telling me that Roger was in big trouble and me going to pray for him would probably make no difference. But knowing I could not let Carol and Roger down I reluctantly accepted their invitation with a broad smile but with much trepidation.

Once my surgery was finished I made my way slowly to the hospital sensing God's rebuke at my reluctance and my lack of faith. The words of Jesus in Matthew 25 came to my mind, 'for I was hungry and you gave me food, I was thirsty and you gave me drink, I was a stranger and you welcomed me, I was naked and you clothed me, *I was sick and you visited me*, I was in prison and you came to me' (my emphasis). By the time I reached the hospital I felt suitably chastised. I had immense peace knowing that God's presence was with us as we walked onto the ward. In the intensive care unit, Carol and I sat by Roger's bed and we prayed a simple prayer, asking God to come and heal Roger and restore him to full health. Roger's doctors indicated to Carol that they were expecting him to die within 24 hours. As we came out of the ward, we sat together on the stairs and Carol said, 'You're not going to let him die, are you?' – as if there was anything I could do about it!

Miraculously, from that point in time Roger made a slow recovery and returned to full health, suffering no lasting damage. He recovered consciousness just two days after Carol and I had prayed with him. Following his discharge, I readmitted him to the hospital twice, firstly with a deep vein thrombosis and then with a pulmonary embolus from his thrombosis. The slightly stormy recovery did not diminish the sense of God's intervention and Carol and Roger made a commitment to Christ having discovered for themselves the God of miracles.

One of the greatest challenges that we face as Christians, trying to respond to the call of Jesus, is to overcome the tyranny of 'having no time'. The pace of life in modern society is bizarre. Another common 'ailment' that I encounter in General Practice, is that of people coming in saying they feel 'tired all the time'. So common is this nowadays, that it is actually ranked as a diagnosis, known as the TATT syndrome. The causes for this however are not fully understood. Certainly, there may be many contributing medical factors including the prevalence of viral illness leading to post-viral fatigue, and the huge increase in depression. Indeed, the feeling of being persistently tired is one of the many symptoms of depression. But I feel sure that one of the other main reasons for many people feeling persistently tired is that we are all trying to pack far too much into our lives, simply because it is possible to do so. Modern society demands it.

Not so very long ago, a trip to London from Southampton would have taken place over several days. We would have travelled to work on foot because it would have been in the local vicinity. Shopping would have been done daily and much of the time spent at home would have been washing clothes by hand, cleaning, mending and doing simple everyday chores. Communication with others was face-to-face or by letter. With the amazing progression of society, modern systems of transportation, labour-saving devices, and new means of communication, it is now possible to pack into one day what would previously have been impossible in a week. We travel to London and back again, we speak to ten people on the telephone, making important decisions about their lives and ours, we go off and do the week's shopping, put the washing in the machine and e-mail another six people who are demanding our response. With the wonder of our modern society, we face the ever-increasing assaults on our minds. This is a by-product of progress and we must be wary of being consumed by it.

In a *Times* article in October 2001, Peggy Noonan, a former speech writer to Presidents Reagan and Bush Senior wrote this:

> *We have no time! Is it that way for you? Everyone seems so busy. Once, a few years ago, I sat on the Spanish steps in Rome. Suddenly I realised that everyone, all the people going up and down the steps, was hurrying along on his or her way somewhere. I thought everyone is doing something. On the streets of Manhattan they hurry along and I think, everyone is busy. I do not think I have seen anyone amble, except at a summer place, in a long time.*
>
> *All our splendour, our comfort, takes time to pay for. And affluence wants to increase: it carries within it an unspoken command: more! Affluence is like nature which always moves towards new life. Nature does its job; affluence enlists us to do it. ...*
>
> *... So we work. The more you have, the more you need, the more you work and plan. This is odd in part because of all the spare time we should have. We don't, after all, have to haul water from the 'crick'. We don't have to kill an antelope for*

dinner. I can microwave a Lean Cuisine meal in four minutes and eat it in five. I should have a lot of extra time – more, say, than a cave woman. And yet I feel I do not. And I think: that cave woman watching the antelope turn on the spit, she was probably happily day-dreaming about how shadows played on the walls of her cave. She had time.

*　　It is not just work. We all know the application of Parkinson's Law, that work expands to fill the time allotted to complete it. This isn't new. But this is: so many of us feel that we have no time to cook and serve a lovely three-course dinner, to write a long thoughtful letter, to tutor ever so patiently the child. But other generations, not so long ago, did. And we have more time-saving devices than they did. We invented new technologies so that work could be done more efficiently and quickly. We wished (work) done more quickly so we could have more leisure time. (Wasn't that the plan? Or was it to increase our productivity?). But we have less leisure time, it seems, because these technologies encroach on our leisure time.*[2]

In exposing the tyranny of time within current society, Peggy Noonan alluded to the next great tyranny of our time: the pressure to work more in order to earn more. Until fairly recently it was the norm for just one member of the family unit to work. As time has progressed opportunities have increased and the amount of chores in the home has lessened meaning that more and more people have been able to go out to work. In fact, opportunities have not only arisen to enable us to work but the economic situation 'demands' that we work. One family wage is insufficient to cover the costs of the modern home, as house prices continue to rise faster than salaries. Even our children find part-time jobs as soon as possible in order to enjoy the benefits of financial freedom alongside their peers.

The advancement and progression of our modern society is, of course, very far from being all bad. The huge improvement of life expectancy brought about by the simple provision of clean water, improved living and working environments and the amazing advances of medical science, are some of the great privileges of the modern age. The time challenges that have been brought about through the advances noted previously, have also brought with them wonderful new opportunities for all of us.

The challenge for us as Christians is to set all of this in the context of the words of Jesus in the parable the Good Samaritan. If we are to bring a distinctive savour to our modern society we may need to make radical decisions when choosing the pathway for our lives. These decisions may be quite simple, but may bring huge benefits to us. Sheelagh and I have lived in our current home for the past twenty-one years. It is a lovely home, an old Victorian house, which we have slowly renovated and modernised over the time we have been here. The only drawback is that it is sited on one of Southampton's main commuter roads and at times simply getting in and out of the drive can be quite a problem. On the salary that I have earned over the past several years we could have quite easily moved from this house, extended our mortgage, and kept up with the expectations of society in bettering ourselves. However, some time ago we made a conscious decision that we would not continue on the ladder of the ever-extending mortgage, but in fact try and do the opposite and get our mortgage down as quickly as possible. By doing this, I have been able to go part-time in General Practice, giving me back that precious commodity of time, in order to do other things. The 'hardship' of living on a main road is no hardship at all, and is nothing compared to the immense benefit brought about through time regained. We continue to thank God for the provision of a beautiful home, which more than provides for all of our needs, and which is sited amongst a community of wonderful friends. I realise that I am extremely fortunate to have the luxuries of a comfortable house and family. For others this is not the case. However, this was just one simple choice I have made for my life. We all have the opportunity to make simple choices, countering the demands of the modern consumer culture and leading to a distinctive lifestyle.

> *With eyes wide open to the mercies of God, I beg you, my brother's as an act of intelligent worship, to give him your bodies, as a living sacrifice, consecrated to him and acceptable by him. Don't let the world around you squeeze you into its own mould, but let God remould your minds from within, so that you may prove in practice that the plan of God for you is good, meets all his demands and moves towards the goal of true maturity.*
>
> *Romans 12:1–2, J. B. Phillips*

Christians are distinguished from other men
neither by country, nor language,
nor the customs which they observe.
For they neither inhabit cities of their own,
nor employ a peculiar form of speech,
nor lead a life which is marked out by any singularity

They dwell in their own country,
but simply as sojourners.
As citizens, they share in all things with others,
and yet endure all things as if foreigners.
Every foreign land is to them as their native country,
And every land of their birth as a land of strangers ...
They are in the flesh but
They do not live after the flesh.

They pass their days on earth,
but they are citizens of heaven.
They obey the prescribed laws,
And at the same time surpass the laws by their lives.

They love all men,
and are persecuted by all ...
They are poor,
yet make many rich ...
To sum up all in one word –
what a soul is in the body, that are Christians in the world.

Taken from a letter to Diognetes, circa AD 150

4

A Heart of Compassion

The parable of the Good Samaritan introduces us to an attitude of the heart which is fundamental to the Christian life. 'But a Samaritan, as he journeyed, came to where he was; and when he saw him he had *compassion*' (my emphasis). The word here, translated as compassion, comes from a strange Greek word *splagchnizethai*. This Greek verb is derived from the word *splagchna*, which means from 'the noble viscera' – the heart, the lungs, the liver and the intestines. Even in medicine today the adjective splanchnic is used to denote 'of the viscera, or intestinal', and within our bodies we have a splanchnic artery. This ancient Greek verb, literally means to be deeply moved in one's 'bowels' or, perhaps, more literally in today's language, to be moved to the depths of one's being. The Greeks often thought that particular abdominal or bodily organs were associated with the seat of different emotions and even in our language today such phrases as 'feeling it in your bones', 'venting your spleen', or having 'butterflies in your tummy' – perpetuate this line of thinking.

Strangely, in ancient Greece, the prevailing thought was that a divine being should be devoid of all feeling and emotion. Stoicism, founded under the tutelage of the philosopher Zeno some 250 years before Christ, took up this thinking and taught that if man was to attain to any sense of moral worth, he too should become devoid of emotion and accept his fate with sternness and tranquillity of mind. In our language today we still use the word stoical, which by definition means to be indifferent to pleasure or pain. The ancient Greeks certainly would not have recognised a god who was 'moved with compassion.' However, an emotionless, unfeeling god is not the God who reveals himself to us in the Bible. The gospels, and the life of Jesus Christ, reveal a God of compassion, a God who feels intensely for his children, a God who stopped at nothing to rescue his children from a lost eternity.

The Samaritan was moved with compassion. This profound compassion is translated on only twelve other occasions, all found in the gospels and attributed solely to the attitudes and actions of either Jesus or his Father. This makes the use of the word 'compassion' here all the more remarkable. Despite coming from the same Greek derivative as the 'compassion' displayed by God, this is the only time the word is attributed to men.

A study of the occasions on which this deep compassion was displayed, reveals much about the father heart of God and its expression through the life of Jesus. In telling parables concerning his Father, Jesus revealed the compassionate heart of God to the lost. In Matthew 18: 27, in the parable of forgiveness, the 'Master' was moved with compassion for the servant who could not pay his debt. In the parable of the Prodigal Son in Luke 15 (a parable we shall return to in chapter nine) Jesus displays an even greater depth of God's heart of compassion. When the father saw his lost and returning son (15:20), he was 'moved with compassion, and ran and embraced and kissed him.' These parables display God's tender longing to embrace each of us in love and forgiveness. We can almost hear his heartbeat, yearning to bring us to the truth of knowing and experiencing his compassion.

This same compassion was displayed in the life of Jesus. Jesus, too, was moved by the lost souls of people (Mt. 9:36), but he was also moved with their brokenness (Lk. 7:13), their sickness (Mt. 14:14; Mk. 1:41; 9:22), their hunger (Mt. 5:32; Mk. 8:2) and their need (Mt. 20:34). It is interesting to note that within all of these references, being moved with compassion is not simply a feeling or an emotion: it is always followed by an action. Compassion is gut-wrenching; it cannot leave us unmoved. The Greek derivative of the word compassion conveys this intensity of feeling which literally stirs us deep within, and *demands* that an action must follow. Jesus prayed for the lost, healed the sick, fed the hungry and raised the dead. If we are to take up the challenge of Jesus that he outlined through the parable of the Good Samaritan, then our compassion cannot be confined to warm feelings, but needs to be expressed through activity. The use of this 'compassion' in the parable of the Good Samaritan reveals how much God wants the church to be an ongoing demonstration of his tender heart of love. We are constantly drawn back to living out our faith through actions.

Our own English word compassion is derived from the Latin *cum pati*, meaning 'with feeling' or 'to feel with'. If we are to express God's heart of compassion to those who are hurting we must allow ourselves to feel with them, to be empathetic (same root derivation). 'Feeling with' people can be expressed in many ways. It may be by listening, in communication (both verbal and non-verbal) through touch, or simply by just being with them. In his book entitled *Compassion* Henri Nouwen wrote this:

When do we receive real comfort and consolation? Is it when someone teaches us how to think or act? Is it when we receive advice about where to go or what to do? Is it when we hear words of reassurance and hope? Sometimes, perhaps. But what really counts is that in moments of pain or suffering someone stays with us. More important than any particular action or word of advice is the simple presence of someone who cares.[1]

Several years ago I was invited to speak at a conference in Scotland. As I normally work as an anaesthetist at the local hospital on a Friday afternoon, I left my practice on the Friday lunchtime. Being away for the weekend, meant that I was out of touch with the events that were to unfold. Arriving back at the practice on the Monday morning I was greeted by the tragic news of the death of one of my eighteen-year-old patients, who, despite seeking medical attention, had died of a very rare complication of sinusitis. When I went to see his parents I felt absolutely helpless, with a sense of having nothing to offer them and a feeling that somehow I had let them down. As they recounted the tragedy of the death of their son I simply wept with them in their grief. I did not feel that I was able to offer them anything. And yet since that time I have had a most wonderful relationship with them as a family. Simply being there was an expression of compassion, one tiny gesture which brought about the lasting benefit of a deeper relationship.

Spending time just being with people is the beginning of expressing God's heart of compassion; we can add to this by 'feeling with' them in other ways. Some months ago a young man who was extremely depressed came in to see me. His life seemed to be a complete mess. He left school with no qualifications and very quickly began drinking heavily and then became addicted to drugs. Starting on cannabis, he soon progressed to injecting hard drugs and soon got into trouble with the police. As I listened to his sad story I started to feel that there must be a reason for his downward spiral and began to probe into his life at school and his childhood to see if there was a problem that had led to this. It did not take long before he began to open up. He told me how he had been the victim of terrible bullying at school. Tragically, this bullying had been ignored by his teachers, despite his cries for help. It had destroyed his confidence and his self-esteem. In trying to escape the pain of his ordeals he had taken to drinking and this had led to the downward spiral of drug taking and lawlessness.

I sat and listened to this story, which (unfortunately for my other patients) took far longer than the ten-minute appointment that he had been allocated. At the end of the consultation, although I had prescribed some medication, I felt that I had done very little for him. However, when he got up he offered his hand and I shook it. I looked up into his tear-filled eyes, and he simply thanked me for listening. I was the first person that he had ever talked to about his problem.

About a year ago, a forty-year-old lady came into my surgery, and she was also feeling very low and depressed. She had come asking for anti-depressants, but I began to ask her why she was feeling so low. Over the course of the next ten minutes she began to tell me about her life. She was unemployed, not particularly because she was unfit to work, but because she was required to be at home with her extremely anxious father who made impossible demands on her time. Alongside this, she helped care for her disabled brother. She began to describe her life as being like a modern-day slave having absolutely no time for herself. She never had time to go out, to make friends or to have any kind of social life; she felt trapped in the situation, caring too much to walk away. The sadness in her eyes conveyed her deep sense of grief and I began to 'feel with her'. The enormity of her problems at home again left me feeling helpless as though I had nothing to offer. I wrote her a prescription for anti-depressants. However, as she got up to go, I broke all the rules of General Practice and said 'Do you mind if I give you a hug?' With a simple hug I looked down at her to say goodbye. With tears filling her eyes she said 'I can't tell you how much that meant to me.' Then she left.

Another elderly lady came in to surgery one day; she had broken her ankle a year or so earlier and now had developed arthritis in the joint. On days, the pain was unbearable. I had referred her back to the Orthopaedic surgeons and to a rheumatologist, but they had no lasting cures for her pain. In despair she said, 'Doctor, isn't there anything you can do?' I had little to offer her medically, but I could pray for her. I sought her permission to pray and she readily agreed. Holding her hands and praying a short prayer, I simply asked God to touch her. When I had finished praying I got up with her, moving to open the door. She stopped me. Holding back her tears she said, 'Doctor, can I give you a kiss?' (I'm happy to say that this does not happen often in my surgeries.) God had touched her. She still hobbled away, but she had simply felt that somebody cared, 'feeling with her' in her pain.

Our need to feel valued is a God given need. Taking time to 'feel with people' – whether it is just by being there, by listening, through a simple hug or through our actions we express a sense of value and worth. Through his acts of compassion, his healing and miracles, we see the value that Jesus placed on each and every life, however sinful and broken. His expressions of love were unreserved, unconditional and extended to all.

In Luke 19 we read of Jesus entering the fashionable town of Jericho, intending just to pass through. Looking on from the crowd, but from the vantage point high up in a tree, was a despised and hated man, a tax collector called Zaccheus. The rich tax collector was spurned and rejected by the crowd of townsfolk. In this sinful man Jesus saw something of value, and to the amazement of the crowd reached out in friendship to Zaccheus with the words 'I *must* stay at your house today' (my emphasis) (19:5). By imparting a sense of worth to Zaccheus, Jesus saw his heart was opened to the salvation of God.

By recounting stories from my General Practice life, I do not want to give you the impression that I am always a kind, compassionate and caring doctor. On many days, nothing could be further from the truth! I can be moody, temperamental and irritable, especially if I think people have trivial complaints and are wasting my time. On the football field, if I get a bad tackle or perceive an injustice, the red mist can descend, and it's not a pretty sight. I am no different to anybody else; whatever our failings and weaknesses, we all need God's grace, forgiveness and discipline to make it through life. Developing a heart of compassion is a discipline of the Christian life and expressing God's heart of compassion may not come easily to us. Taking time to engage with people is something that I constantly have to learn. As a child, I was in some ways very shy and always found eye contact very embarrassing. Consequently when I spoke to people I tended to look past them or at a spot somewhere on their forehead in order to avoid eye contact. Over the past few years I have realised how important eye contact is in engaging with people, as are gestures of acceptance and value such as shaking hands and affording people your full attention. Henri Nouwen cites G. K. Chesterton as he describes the life of St Francis of Assisi.

What gave him extraordinary personal power was this; that from the Pope to the beggar, from the Sultan of Syria in his pavilion to the ragged robbers crawling out of the wood, there was never a man who looked into those brown burning eyes without being certain that Francis Bernardone was really interested in him, in his own individual life from the cradle to the grave; that he himself was being valued and being taken seriously, and not merely added to the spoils of some social policy or the names in some clerical document ... He treated the whole mob of men as a mob of Kings.[2]

Engaging people with eye contact is a discipline that I have had to learn. With such very simple gestures, we can impart value to another. Last year I was heartbroken when a close friend of mine committed suicide. James had long suffered with the terrible affliction of manic depression and had battled bravely with the disease. Many years ago he had made a commitment to Christ and, although his faith had remained secure, he had not been a regular attender at church. Our friendship had continued through the mutual love of sport, and for years we played football together on a Friday evening, along with many other men from the church. After the football, we would often come back and sit and relax with a beer. Two years ago, James and I and two other friends from our football group, went skiing together in France. Although James had never previously been skiing, he was a natural, and within a space of four days was skiing down slopes marked red, the second most difficult slopes on the pistes. Every evening, relaxing over a meal, we would laugh about the exploits of the day, but we also talked a lot about our faith.

At the time of his death James was living with his business partner, Tony. Unbeknown to me, James had left specific letters for a number of people, and I was surprised that I was one of them. When Tony delivered the letter, he told me how James had expressed to him the affection that he had felt for me, and he said something which I found amazing. Apparently, one of the things that James appreciated in our relationship was that when I arrived on the football field, I would shake him by the hand and look him in the eye, before catching up on events of the week. Such a simple gesture of engagement had made a profound impact.

If we are to grow in living the compassionate lifestyle, then compassion must become a discipline alongside our other Christian disciplines; it is a discipline that begins through our Bible reading and through prayer. The compassionate heart of God was expressed in Jesus Christ who 'had to be made like His brethren in every respect' (Heb. 2:17). Though he was rich he became poor, and in his poverty he was able to 'feel with' people. Through the cross he suffered the brokenness, rejection and loneliness that so many people encounter today. The Scriptures reveal this compassionate heart. Prayer grounds our daily attempts to lead a compassion-filled life. By turning our thoughts in prayer to the needs of others, we give opportunity to place value on another person's life, to esteem them above ourselves. Thoughtfulness concerning others is a characteristic so lacking in our society today and when things go wrong in life, or when a careless word is uttered how often do we hear it said 'he was so thoughtless'?

My brother Richard is a very thoughtful person, and I have tried to learn much from him. In the past, at birthdays or at Christmas, he has given the most amazing presents. They had obviously been chosen with much thought, showing he had remembered a conversation from months earlier (that might have revealed your likes or dislikes) and his presents, chosen with such care, not only expressed his thoughtfulness, but also the value that he placed on the recipient.

Richard's thoughtfulness presents to me a challenge to my discipline of compassion. In our devotional lives we have the opportunity to bring our thoughts to God. Each day we can ask him: Is there anybody that needs my help today? What are the needs of my friends, my family and my work colleagues? Do I need to spend time with somebody, to listen, to feel with, and to give to them? The compassionate acts of Jesus often stemmed from, or led to, times of prayer (Mk. 1:35–40; Mt. 9:35–37; Mk. 6:30–46). If we are to convey God's heart of compassion and kindness to a hungry world we must begin through the simple disciplines of the Christian faith. Thomas Cahill writes:

> As we stand now at the entrance to the third millennium since Jesus, we can look back over the horrors of Christian history, never doubting for an instant that if Christians had put kindness [compassion] ahead of devotion to good order, theological correctness, and our own justifications – if we had followed in the humble footsteps of the heretical Samaritan, who was willing to wash someone else's wounds, rather than in the self-regarding steps of the priest and the immaculate steps of the Levite – the world we inhabit would be a very different one.[3]

As we press on with our journey to the heart of God, let us combine the discipline of devotion to the discipline of compassion. Let us try to consider daily the needs of others, getting in tune with the whispers of God's heart as we kneel at his feet. As Brennan Manning says, 'Our culture says that ruthless competition is the key to success. Jesus says that ruthless compassion is the purpose of our journey.'[4]

If you have gotten anything at all out of following Christ, if his love has made any difference in your life, if being in a community of the spirit means anything to you, if you have a heart, if you **care** *– then do me a favor: agree with each other, love each other, be deep-spirited friends. Don't push your way to the front; don't sweet-talk your way* *to the top. Put yourself aside, and help others get ahead. Don't be obsessed with getting your own advantage. Forget yourselves long enough to lend a helping hand.*

Think of yourselves the way Christ Jesus thought of himself. He had equal status with God but did not think so much of himself that he had to cling to all the advantages of that status no matter what. Not at all. When the time came he set aside the privileges of deity and took on the status of a slave, became **human!** *Having become human he stayed human. It was an incredibly humbling process. He didn't claim special privileges. Instead, he lived a selfless, obedient life and then died a selfless, obedient death – and the worst kind of death at that – crucifixion.*

Because of that obedience, God lifted him high and honored him far beyond anyone or anything, ever, so that all created beings in heaven and on earth even those long ago dead and buried – will bow in worship before this Jesus Christ, and call out in praise that he is the Master of all, to the glory of God the Father.

Philippians 2:1–11, The Message

5

Mercy Triumphs over Judgement

About ten years ago, in the early days of Care Centres Network, I was asked to speak at a day conference in the Midlands. At the time I felt it was important that I emphasise the need for church involvement and backing for people wanting to start pregnancy counselling centres. At the end of the morning, a lady came up to me and said, 'Phil, I really agree with you that we need church backing for our project, but I went to our pastor and explained that I wanted to start a pregnancy counselling centre, and when I asked for his backing he said, 'I don't want those sort of people in my church.' I felt shocked and angry; what sort of people did he mean? Could he mean sinners like you and me? Despite having an excellent day at the conference, the only thing I could think about on my journey home was this one comment and I could feel myself getting more and more angry about this. What right had he to judge these women? Just who did he think he was? As I drove home stewing on his remarks, it suddenly dawned on me – I was just as bad: I was now judging him.

Only a few years earlier, God had spoken to me very clearly because of my judgemental attitudes. Again, this had risen in the area of abortion. Shelley was a young woman in her early twenties who was in a stable relationship, and she had come in to my surgery one day absolutely radiant.

She proudly announced that she was pregnant, and I spent quite some time talking with her about what would happen to her through the pregnancy. We talked about what she would need to do, I told her when her baby was going to be due, and then when we would like to see her again. As she was only six weeks into the pregnancy we would not need to see her for a further four to six weeks and she left the surgery with an appointment for that time. It was quite a surprise, therefore, to see Shelley's name on my list only a few days later. As she came through the door her demeanour could not have been more different. 'Doctor, I want you to arrange for me to have an abortion.' I was shocked. What had gone wrong? Shelley said, 'When I went home, I told my boyfriend that I was pregnant. He said, "Get rid of it; I don't want a baby yet. If you don't get rid of it I am leaving." I don't want to lose my boyfriend, doctor. I just can't go on with this pregnancy.' Shelley's mind was completely closed to any discussion.

A few days later I was on call for the practice and late into the evening a call came through saying that Shelley had requested a visit. The medical telephonist who had taken the call merely related that a young woman had telephoned to say that she had been discharged from hospital that day, having had an abortion, and she was now bleeding very heavily. At first I just felt very sad that Shelley had gone ahead with the abortion, but as I drove across town I could feel myself becoming more and more angry and thinking really horrible thoughts such as 'Well, this just serves her right.' I pulled up outside the block of flats where she lived. It was dark and the roads were deserted; I was tired and I was very angry. I turned off the car engine and just sat for a moment to try to calm down. It was then that I began to sense God's presence. I felt God speaking to my heart, saying: 'What right have you to come and judge this woman? Just consider your life at the moment.' As I sat in the car I began to think about my life: my upbringing, my caring family, the opportunities I had had in life, the education I had received my marriage, my children, and the happiness that God had given me. Then I thought of Shelley. She had none of these privileges, and even the love she thought she had, she was desperately frightened of losing.

I felt so chastened by God that I could not go in to see Shelley for some minutes but had to sit and pray and ask God's forgiveness for my terrible attitude. When I did go in to see her, Shelley was sitting in bed quietly weeping. As I entered the room she said to me, 'I am so sorry doctor. I bet you are thinking this just serves me right!' As I sat on the end of the bed, I could honestly reply to her, that no, that was not what I was thinking. I admitted Shelley back into hospital and I went home to bed having learned a very important lesson.

As Christians we have absolutely no right to judge anybody. God alone is our righteous judge: even Jesus did not pass judgement on others. In Acts 17:31 we find that God 'has fixed a day when He will judge the world in righteousness.' In Genesis 19 the Scriptures give us a picture of a sinful world in the story of Sodom and Gomorrah, cities so evil that they were overthrown by God in an act of judgement. Yet at the same time as destroying these cities God reaches down in mercy and kindness to the family of Lot and rescues them from the destruction. 2 Peter 2:6 tells us that this is an *example* to those who would be ungodly. In Hebrews 9:27 we are told that it is 'appointed for men to die and *after that* comes judgement' (my emphasis).

I find that we, in the church, are all too ready to pass judgement on people because of their perceived sin. Twenty years ago when the AIDS epidemic was breaking out, I commonly heard comments amongst Christians that 'AIDS is God's judgement on homosexuals.' A pastor friend of mine visited Los Angeles shortly after an earthquake had brought down several flyovers crushing cars underneath and killing many people. Whilst he was there, my friend had heard that some churches were saying that this was 'God's judgement on the city of Los Angeles for the sin of that city.'

As we look through the scriptures I see no justification at all for such statements.* If we look to our example in Christ we find one who did not come to judge the world but to extend mercy and hope, and new life to those who would turn to him. As for many Christians, John 3:16 was the first verse that I learned from the Bible: 'For God so loved the world that He gave His only son, that whoever believes in Him should not perish but have eternal life.' If only I had learned verse seventeen at the same time; 'For God sent His son into the world not to judge the world, but that through him the world might be saved.' When faced with the woman caught in adultery, a story I shall return to later, Jesus said to her 'neither do I condemn [judge] you; go and do not sin again.' Again in John 12:47 Jesus says, 'If anyone hears my sayings and does not keep them, I do not judge him; for I did not come to judge the world but to save the world.'

To me, therefore, the epidemic of AIDS merely represents a consequence of permissive society, and is in no way the judgement of God. On the contrary; I believe we are living in an age of the God's bountiful mercy, mercy that he freely showers on his ill-deserving children. The book of 2 Peter tells us that God 'is not wishing for any to perish, but all

---

* The only place that I can find where men are called upon to make a judgement is a special responsibility given to the leaders of the church when a member of the congregation continues in a lifestyle of sin (1 Cor. 5:12).

to come to a knowledge of the truth' (3:9). We find God's heart reflected in Jesus in his passion for the lost. In the last chapter we saw how Jesus was moved with compassion by the lost nature of the individual life, and despite at times being overwhelmed by the crowds, he would reach out to them with kindness, mercy and hope.

As Christians we have read the gospels many times and noted how Jesus reserved his strongest words for the Pharisees, the 'whitewashed tombs' (Mt. 23:27) who 'laid heavy burdens on other men whilst not lifting a finger for themselves' (Lk. 11:46). We talk with scorn of the judgemental Pharisees and yet we often behave exactly like them. It can be very tempting as Christians when we try to live our lives by a set of values that are ascribed to our faith, that we then start to make judgements about people who lead their lives differently to us. How soon we forget where we have come from and how merciful God has been towards us. I have often heard Christians describe life 'in the church' and life 'in the world'. In some ways this is scriptural in that Jesus prays for us to 'be in the world but not of the world' (Jn. 17:14–16). However, what we must not do is think that as Christians we have a monopoly on God. God does not have any favourites, whether Christian or non-Christian. He loves all humankind with an equal intensity, and as God's representatives on earth we should reflect this passion and mercy for all. God has blessed Sheelagh and I with four beautiful children who, at the time of my writing, are all at different stages in their spiritual development. Our son, James, is working in church outreach in Spain. Two of my three daughters rarely come to church and at the present time seem to have little enthusiasm to do so. Now the question is: do I love any of my children more or less because of this? Of course not. I love my four children passionately. Their lives and their actions may please me or displease me, but I can never ever stop loving them. If these feelings are such for an earthly father how much more true is it of our Heavenly Father, who loves all men without partiality? Jesus himself said these words:

> *If you love those who love you, what credit is that to you? For even sinners love those who love them. And if you do good to those who do good to you, what credit is that to you? For even sinners do the same. And if you lend to those from whom you hope to receive, what credit is that to you? Even sinners lend to sinners, to receive as much again. But love your enemies, and do good, and lend, expecting nothing in return; and your reward will be great, and you will be sons of the Most High;* for he is kind to the ungrateful and the selfish. *Be merciful, even as your father is merciful. Judge not and you will not be judged* ... (Lk. 6:32–37), my emphasis.

There are many areas in life in which we casually pass judgement on other people without giving it a second thought. We very often pass comment, gossip, or speak badly of others, and criticise their behaviour. By painting a poor picture of one person to another, we seek to do them down, whilst at the same time promoting ourselves in a good light. It was just such attitudes in the Pharisees that Jesus abhorred. The book of James tells us

> not to speak evil against one another. He that speaks evil against a brother or judges his brother, speaks evil against the law and judges the law but if you judge the law, you are not a doer of the law but a judge, there is one law giver and judge, he who is able to save and to destroy. But who are you that you should judge your neighbour? (Jas. 4:11–12)

In the same book of James we are exhorted not to discriminate or judge people by their appearances (Jas. 2:1–7). Some years ago one of our surgery premises was repeatedly vandalised over a period of several months by young men from the estate. We would arrive at work in the morning to find windows smashed, drainpipes ripped off the wall and tiles broken on the surgery roof. Not only did this prove expensive to repair but it soon became clear that we were not going to be able to insure the building if the vandalism continued. In the end we had to spend a considerable amount of money putting shutters over all the windows and making the building as secure as possible against vandalism. Often we would leave the surgery and see the young lads we believed were causing the trouble, dressed in long parka coats, with beanie hats pulled down over their heads.

A few weeks later my son, James, and I were walking down on a Friday evening to play football with our friends from the church. It was a dark, cold winter evening. On our way down to the sports centre we passed another group of lads dressed in long parka coats and beanie hats. As we passed, one of the lads recognised James, and he grunted a greeting. To me they looked exactly like the lads who had been wrecking our surgery. Once they were out of earshot I turned to James and said, 'They looked like a bunch of no-goods.' James was quick in his rebuke: 'Dad, you shouldn't judge by appearances.' The sports centre where we play football is five miles away from the surgery in the estate. They were not, of course, the same boys damaging the surgery, but in my mind, they looked the same: I had judged them by their appearance. It is so easy when we have had a negative experience in life, to make sweeping generalisations about other people, whether individuals, classes, or even whole races.

Not long after this event, in the run up to Christmas, I was doing an antenatal clinic at the surgery. Tracey, a young girl of fourteen, came for her first antenatal appointment. I was struck by her age – she seemed just a child – the same age as one of my daughters. It would have been so easy to judge her appearance and make comment on her lifestyle. When I finished the clinic, I went through to reception where one of our more senior receptionists had been working. When Tracey had left my room, she had gone to make her next appointment. Our receptionist then told me what had happened.

It was so sad with Tracey. When she came to make the appointment at the desk she just hung around and seemed not to want to go home. She said to me, 'Are you working at Christmas?' I replied that I was working up until Christmas, but was not actually working Christmas Day or Boxing Day. 'Oh, you must have to work really hard,' Tracey said. 'My mum don't work hard, she don't do nothing. She just sits in the chair all day and watches the telly'. She looked back at me and said 'Are you a grandma?' I told her I was. 'Ah, I bet you make a lovely grandma.'

It was not difficult to see what Tracey was really saying. Having not experienced the love and care of her own mother, she had gone out and sought love in the only way she had known and had ended up becoming pregnant. Her desperate longing, her heart's desire, was to have a mother who cared, a mother who would be a loving grandmother to her child. How easy it is to pass judgement on people's lives simply through appearances, not knowing the pain and suffering they may have endured.

Angela's Story
Angela, her husband John and their three children had been with our practice for years. I had got to know them all quite well. Angela was a good mum,

caring for the family and working hard, and was always bright and cheerful when she came to see me in surgery. From the outside, her marriage appeared stable and her life secure.

Arriving in surgery one morning, I saw Angela's name on my list. When she came through the door, she was clearly not her usual happy self. 'Doctor Clarke,' she said, 'I'm pregnant and I want you to arrange for me to have an abortion.' This seemed incomprehensible. She had three beautiful children whom she loved dearly; surely one more wouldn't be too difficult. As I pressed her for an explanation, she said: 'You don't understand. This is not my husband's baby.'

So that was the problem. Angela had had an affair, and she wanted to have an abortion to save her marriage and spare her children the trauma of seeing their parents split up.

Angela didn't want to talk about it any more; please could I just get on and refer her to hospital. Nothing I could say or do would persuade Angela otherwise. I wrote a letter of referral seeking a further opinion, and Angela had an abortion.*

---

* I know that many GPs who oppose abortion are not comfortable referring women to hospital. My own policy is to write a letter of referral seeking a further opinion, whilst not agreeing with the procedure. I do this for a number of reasons. Firstly, God has given us free choice. This is a basic principle of the Christian faith. God does not interfere with that choice, even though it may lead to separation from him. Abortion is a legal choice. We may not agree with abortion, but we must respect that each person has the right to make their own choices and choose their own destiny. Secondly, though I may not agree with her choice, I want to leave the door open

I didn't see Angela, or any of her family, for the next few months. Then one morning I noticed her name on my list. When she came through the door, I could see she was upset and she broke down in tears. I felt immediately that it was the abortion that was upsetting her. When she confirmed this, I felt quite smug, but my self-righteous satisfaction was soon to evaporate.

Finally Angela regained her composure sufficiently enough to talk. 'It is the abortion I'm upset about, but it's not the way you think. I want to tell you something. I've never told anybody before. My mum is an alcoholic and has been for as long as I can remember. When I was a child she was always drunk, she never did any of the housework or cooked for us, and my sister, brother and I had to look after ourselves 'til dad came in from work. If I was ever upset or ill, I would go to dad, and some nights would climb into his bed. Then he started "touching" me, calling me his special little girl. That was from the age of about six.

'I later found out he had been doing the same to my older sister, who was six years older than me. When my sister was fifteen, she couldn't stand it at home any longer and she left. That left me with my

---

for all of my patients to come back and talk afterwards. If women feel judged by my refusing to help them, they are unlikely to come to me afterwards if they run into problems. Thirdly, if consultants only receive letters of approval from referring GPs, there remains no challenge to their actions. I hope that by constantly disagreeing with their actions, I remain a provocation and a challenge to their thinking.

brother, who was four years older than me. Not long after my sister left, my brother started to abuse me, only his abuse was much worse than my dad. He made me have sex with him, at least twice a week, and as time went on, he used me as his sex slave, experimenting on me for his sexual gratification. This went on for ten years until I was nineteen.'

When I asked Angela why she had not tried to resist her brother, she said. 'When I was nine, I was not able to resist him. I couldn't go to my mum 'cos she was always drunk. Despite what my dad did to me, I started to feel sorry for him 'cos he was working but having to look after himself. I hated what my brother was doing to me, but life was so awful at home, I just thought it was better to keep quiet.'

Angela thought her misery would end when her brother announced he was getting married. However, unbelievably, within two weeks of his marriage, he returned and the abuse started again. Now Angela was desperate! She just had to get away. Now in her late teens, she hatched a plot to escape the abuse. She would go out and find a man, any man, make herself attractive to him and hopefully he would want to marry her. This was the way Angela met her husband. 'I never really loved him,' she said. 'Of course I liked him but there were no feelings of love.'

Incredibly, even after Angela's marriage, her brother came round while her husband was out, and tried to abuse her again. This time she resisted, saying she would tell her husband, but the nightmare had not gone away. Only now, she was locked in a loveless marriage.

Angela kept her head down, cared for her new husband and soon got pregnant. Over just a few years, she had three children, all girls, whom she adored. As the girls grew up however, Angela's life became harder. The pain of the past clung to her: she was unfulfilled in her marriage and as well as caring for her own husband and family, she went every day to her parents where she would clean and prepare meals for them too.

Reaching a low point in her life, Angela finally confided in an old male school friend. 'He understood; he gave me a hug. One thing led to another,' she said. 'I ended up sleeping with him. We only did it once and I got pregnant. Just my luck. For the first time in my life I felt someone loved me.'

Finally Angela said, 'That was when I came to you and asked for an abortion.' I didn't know what to say. The sadness of her story overwhelmed me.

Angela's story taught me again that things are not always what they seem. It is so easy to look at the bare facts – an affair that led to an abortion – and pass judgement. I had no right to do that. Hearing the whole story helps me to understand, yet I should not always need to know the whole story.

Since Angela told me her story, I have spoken to her more about her abortion. The circumstances of her life did not make the abortion right, but at the time it seemed like her only choice. Angela herself has come to regret it. 'If only I had listened to you and taken more time over the decision,' she said. After the abortion, her marriage broke down anyway. Her husband moved away and she began a new life with the father of her lost child. 'We still cry about it together,' she said. 'If anything good can come out of this, it would be to try to make women take more time before they go ahead with an abortion.'

The 'holier than thou' behaviour of the Pharisees was the behaviour for which Jesus reserved his sternest words and when he saw the same attitude amongst his own disciples, he rebuked them severely. In Luke chapter 9 we see Jesus passing through a village of the Samaritans where he was turned away. His disciples were ready to call down fire from heaven 'but he turned and rebuked them, and they went on to another village' (54–55). Jesus may have been rejected by the Samaritans, but it was not the disciples' place to pass judgement on them for doing so. In showing his disciples what *not* to do, Jesus revealed to them what they *should* do. From this same chapter in Luke's gospel we see that Jesus had 'set His face to go to Jerusalem' (51). He knew his destiny; he knew the horror of what lay before him. In the Garden of Gethsemane, he would sweat great drops of blood at the prospect of the terrible pain and death that he would suffer for each one of us. And yet it was on this journey, during the last few days of his life that he passed through Jericho, the rich and fashionable town on the plains below Jerusalem.

And so back to Zaccheus. In Chapter 19, Luke tells us that Jesus 'was just passing through' (1). His eye was caught by a small man who had climbed a tree, whose name was Zaccheus. Even for the prosperous town of Jericho, Zaccheus was extremely rich. It is not clear from the Scripture how Jesus knew that it was Zacchaeus. It may simply have been that, as he was walking into the town with the crowd, he noticed a man climbing a tree. 'Who is that man there climbing the tree?' he might have said. 'Oh that is Zacchaeus' came the reply. 'Let's keep away from him; he is a nasty piece of work, the local tax collector.' Or perhaps Jesus just sensed God speaking and knew who Zaccheus was. We certainly know that the crowd hated Zaccheus because when Jesus did come to him and called him down from the tree, the crowd 'murmured against Him' (7). What incredible love Jesus shows to this hated man. Knowing that he was on the final journey of his life, knowing that he had just a few days to live, and intending to pass through Jericho, he took time to stop and speak to the most despised man in town. Moreover, in an incredible act of friendship he said to Zaccheus, 'I *must* come to your house today' (my emphasis). In the Jewish tradition, dining at the table together is recognition of friendship, acceptance and love. Despite just having days to live, Jesus saw this as his priority.

Kenneth Bailey writes

> *In the East today, as in the past, a nobleman may feed any number of lesser needy persons as a sign of his generosity, but he does not eat with them. However, when guests are 'received' the one receiving the guests eats with them. The meal is a special sign of acceptance. The host affirms this by showering his guests with a long series of compliments to which the guest must respond. Jesus is set forth ... as engaging in some such social relationship with publicans and sinners. Small wonder the Pharisees were upset.*
>
> *In addition to 'eating with sinners' there is the possibility that Jesus was himself hosting sinners. The accusation, 'This one receives sinners and eats with them,' is closely paralleled to Mark 2:15. In this Marcan text Jesus is clearly the host for the meal. The same is true in Luke 15:2.*[1]

Whether Jesus was invited by Zaccheus, or whether he invited himself to the tax collector's home, his actions would have offended some in the crowd. What is clear from the text is that Jesus extended his hand of unconditional acceptance and friendship to a man who was despised and hated.

From the response that Jesus got from Zaccheus, it is obvious that as a tax collector, he had stolen from and defrauded many people. The crowd probably wanted Jesus to expose Zaccheus' sin and judge his lifestyle accordingly. Their murmurings against Jesus revealed a hardness of heart and their displeasure at Jesus giving the man recognition. Yet simply by befriending and loving this man, and without passing any judgement, Jesus brought about a dramatic conversion in Zaccheus. Many times in the gospels we see the Pharisees condemning Jesus for spending time with tax collectors and sinners, even calling Jesus a *'friend* of tax collectors and sinners' (my emphasis). To have been considered their friend, Jesus would have spent much time in their company, in their homes and around meal tables with them. By doing this he offered them unconditional acceptance and love, choosing to see in them the image of his Father which is found in every human being.

He loved people: no strings attached, without judgement or partiality, never expecting anything from them, but always hoping that through loving them, they would choose to follow him. The rich young ruler who came to Jesus had fulfilled all the Law (Mk. 10:17) but he lacked one thing. When Jesus looked at him he *loved him* (my emphasis), and said to him, 'Go sell what you have and give to the poor and you will have treasure in heaven and come follow me.' Similarly, Jesus displayed the free and unreserved kindness of his love, when he healed the ten lepers. Not only did he approach these outcasts of society, he also made it clear that his love and healing was not conditional on the gratitude of the recipient. All ten were healed: just one returned to thank Jesus. This response clearly saddened him, but it didn't change his attitude or love for them.

As we live out our Christian lives we must seek to learn from the example of Jesus. In our pregnancy counselling centres our counsellors and workers seek to convey unconditional love and acceptance to all our clients without hope of any return or reward. It is not for us to judge the lifestyles of others, but merely to love them, regardless.

The longing that Jesus had for people's lost souls meant that his heart's desire was always for people to follow him. Through following him he would show them God's love and bring them to the glory of eternal life. In the same way, we too may share his desire that people's lives are transformed by the knowledge of the gospel of Christ. However, we have no hidden agenda as we seek to love and care for people through the work of the pregnancy counselling centres. The work of salvation in a person's life is down to God and God alone. As we demonstrate unconditional love and kindness to people, we demonstrate the nature and the heart of God. For some, this will draw them to him. A young single mother who was befriended by Trisha, one of our workers, could not believe the kindness that she received when Trisha babysat her existing children, took round meals for them all and showed her kindness when she needed it most. In wanting to find out why this was happening, she came to church, where she gave her life to God and received mercy and hope for the future.

If you really fulfil the royal law, according to the scripture, 'You shall love your neighbour as yourself' you do well. But if you show partiality, you commit sin, and are convicted by the law as transgressors. For whoever keeps the whole law but fails in one point has become guilty of all of it. For he who said, 'Do not commit adultery,' said also, 'Do not kill.' If you do not commit adultery but do kill, you have become a transgressor of the law. So speak and so act as those who are to be judged under the law of liberty. For judgement is without mercy to one who has shown no mercy; yet mercy triumphs over judgement.

James 2:8–13

6

Full of Grace and Truth

*Early in the morning he came again to the temple; all the
people came to him, and he sat down and taught them.
The scribes and Pharisees brought a woman who had been
caught in adultery, and placing her in the midst they said
to him, 'Teacher, this woman has been caught in the act of
adultery. Now in the law Moses commanded us to stone
such. What do you say about her?' This they said this to
test him that they might have some charge to bring against
him. Jesus bent down and wrote with his finger on the
ground. And as they continued to ask him, he stood up and
said to them, 'Let Him who is without sin among you be the
first to throw a stone at her.' And once more he bent down
and wrote with his finger on the ground. But when they
heard it, they went away, one by one, beginning with the
eldest, and Jesus was left alone with the woman standing
before him. Jesus looked up and said to her, 'Woman, where
are they? Has no one condemned you?' She said, 'No-one
Lord.' And Jesus said, "Neither do I condemn you; go and
do not sin again.'*

John 8:2–11

Jewish law is very explicit about the penalty for those who
are caught committing adultery. Not only is it one of the Ten
Commandments found in Exodus 20, but Leviticus 20:10
states very clearly that 'if a man commits adultery with the

wife of his neighbour, both the adulterer and the adulteress shall be put to death.' It might seem strange, therefore, that the Pharisees brought only the woman to Jesus; no mention is made of the man who was involved in this crime. The hypocrisy of the Pharisees was further made evident by the fact that they merely used this situation as a test for Jesus. They had no real care for the woman or, indeed, for the law itself, they were merely out to fulfil their own agenda, by trying to bring Jesus down.

For the woman who had been caught 'in the very act of adultery' (literal translation), the ordeal must have been terrifying. She too would have known the law that said she faced a certain death. More than this, having been caught in a compromising position, she would probably have been naked or barely clothed. Her sense of fear, shame and guilt would have been all-consuming, and the Pharisees were using her as a pawn in their venomous game. To the Pharisees, this woman had no value at all; her life was worth nothing; for all they cared she could die.

Confronted with this difficult situation, the Pharisees demanded Jesus give an appropriate response. If he simply forgave her, he would be seen as contravening the law. If he upheld the law the woman would die. Faced with the increasing intensity of the Pharisees' demands, Jesus bent down and wrote in the sand. I always used to wonder what Jesus was writing; indeed some authors and song writers have even made suggestions as to what it might have been. Questioning what Jesus was writing, however, simply misses the point of what he was doing. If the Bible had wanted us to know what Jesus wrote, it would have been recorded. By writing in the sand, Jesus averted his eyes from the woman who had been cast in the midst of the crowd. By turning his eyes away from her, he did not compound her sense of guilt and shame. The eyes of the crowd turned their focus away from the woman, and instead their gaze was upon Jesus. This woman had been stripped of a sense of value and worth, not only through her own sin, but also through the judgemental actions of others. Jesus' actions began to give this value and worth back to the woman.

In our pregnancy counselling centres, we see many women battling with the same emotions that were felt by the woman caught in adultery. Often women experience a sense of guilt and shame, anger and fear, sorrow and loss of self-esteem alone like the adulteress brought before Jesus. Many of these women are deserted by their male partners, who walk away as soon as an unexpected pregnancy is confirmed. Through loving women caught up in the trauma of unexpected pregnancy, our counsellors adopt the heart of Jesus. Taking the focus away from guilt, shame and fear, they continuously attempt to restore God's focus of value and worth for every human life.

A lack of self-worth seems to be destructively pervading the lives of so many people today. I am constantly saddened by the number of people I see in surgery who generally feel so devalued by those who are supposed to support and love them. Recently, a middle-aged lady called Alice came in to the surgery following the death of her father. She was, naturally, incredibly sad, and yet her sobbing became almost uncontrollable as she explained that her father had died without ever really affirming his sense of value in his daughter. Alice was an only child, her parents always had very high expectations of her, but nothing she could do for them was ever quite good enough. She constantly struggled to achieve, in the hope that they might be proud of her, but she was never praised for what she did right. She was never valued for who she was; her parents continually criticised her for never quite meeting their expectations. To face the loss of her father without ever hearing those words of

A Heart of Compassion

affirmation, the words 'I love you', was almost too hard for her to bear.

In Matthew chapter 13 there are two short parables likening the Kingdom of God to treasure hidden in a field, and of a merchant finding a pearl of great value. Finding life in God will always have infinite and eternal value for us, yet strangely, it is the immeasurable value that God places on each of us which is reflected in these stories. How can we comprehend the price he paid in the sacrifice of his only Son, Jesus, so that our sins could be forgiven? This sacrifice remains a permanent marker of the value and worth that God places on our lives. Before we were in our mother's womb, God set his love upon us, our names inscribed on the palm of his hand. It is this intensity of value and worth that is at the heart of the work of our care centres.

As we have already seen in chapter 3, the Samaritan sect of northern Judea was hated by the Orthodox Jews. In John's gospel chapter 4 we see Jesus 'had to pass through Samaria.' Jesus was weary from his journey, walking through the heat of the day, and around noon, he sat down by the side of a well. A Samaritan woman came to the well to draw water and Jesus asked her to give him a drink. It would have been strange for an Orthodox Jew to have made such a request. Firstly, she was a Samaritan; secondly she was a woman, and an Orthodox Jew would not have conversed with a Samaritan or a woman. This Samaritan woman had previously had five husbands, and was apparently living with a man who was not her husband. From the perspective of an Orthodox Jew this too would have been frowned upon. The custom of the day did not approve of more than three marriages. Jesus did not condone the woman's sinful life, but neither did he judge her. Simply by speaking to her he had unconditionally accepted her. He valued her. He then went on to reveal himself to her in a way that led not only to her salvation, but to the salvation of many of her village. We are beginning to see that Jesus brought people to know him, not through 'preaching', chastising or judging, but through loving, accepting and valuing.

The story of the woman caught in adultery and the story of the Samaritan woman at the well, reveal the immeasurable and undeserved level of God's kindness that we know as grace. We are all sinners; we all deserve the condemnation and judgement of God: and yet instead of judgement, God continually extends his hand of mercy, compassion and kindness.

> For there is no distinction; since all have sinned and fall short of the glory of God, they are justified by His grace as a gift, through the redemption which is in Christ Jesus (Rom. 3:23)

There is absolutely nothing that any one of us can do to earn our salvation or to impress God through our actions. Simply by being his child, I 'impress' God. Our sin, which originally separated us from God, can be forgiven because of the ultimate price God paid in sacrificing Jesus. As Philip Yancey puts it in his book, *What's So Amazing About Grace?*

> Grace baffles us because it goes against the intuition that everyone has that, in the face of injustice, some price must be paid. A murderer cannot simply go free. A child abuser cannot shrug and say, 'I just felt like it.' Anticipating these objections, Paul stressed that a price has been paid – by God Himself. God gave up His own Son rather than give up on humanity.[1]

When I first read this book I was completely bowled over and came to a fresh understanding of God's love and kindness to each of us. This incredible book helped to open my heart, not only to God's kindness displayed towards me, but the mercy that he longs to extend to all of humankind. In seeking to come to a greater understanding of grace I read this book over and over. However, one of the biggest lessons I learnt about God's grace, was through the life of Justin, one of my patients.

Justin's Story

Having moved up from Bournemouth, Justin came on to my list about five years ago. Although he was a relatively young man, he had multiple medical problems due, in part to his lifestyle and previous alcohol abuse. When his notes arrived from Bournemouth, they were in three large volumes. Rather unfairly, we often describe patients with large volume notes and multiple medical problems as 'heart sink' patients: your heart sinks as you see their name on your list! I am sad to say that initially I felt this way about Justin. Not only were many of his problems self-inflicted, but there seemed to be very little that I could do to help him medically. And Justin was a homosexual.

Seeing Justin's name on my surgery list one morning, my heart sank. However, feeling chastened by God for my inner thoughts, I decided to try to offer Justin a bit more of my time, so that I could get to know him and try and understand his problems. Having recently read Philip Yancey's book I was actually asking God to teach me more about his grace and, hence, I wanted to convey a sense of worth and value to Justin when I saw him.

After I had tried to sort out Justin's immediate medical needs, I started asking him about his life and what had led him into drinking. He then began to tell me the story of his life. As a young boy he had a very traumatic time. At the age of six he discovered that the man living with his mother, whom he had assumed to be his real father, was not his father at all. Between giving birth to his older sister and his two younger siblings, his mother had had an affair. Justin was the result of this illicit relationship. His 'father', whilst forgiving his mother, resented Justin and had made his life hell; he was physically and sexually abused by this man. Bearing the bruises of one of his many beatings, Justin's plight was discovered by his grandmother who reported the family to social services. Justin was taken into care and placed in a children's home 'for disturbed children' which was run by a church denomination. Unbelievably, he was sexually abused again whilst in this home, first by the older boys and then by the gardener.

At sixteen Justin returned to his home town and lived with his other grandmother who was the only one of his family who really expressed any love towards him. By now, Justin had accepted that he was homosexual and he openly confessed this to his grandmother. He began working on the buses and quickly became involved in the local gay scene. In his late teens he contracted syphilis, but this was not to be diagnosed for a further seven years, by which time he had suffered irreparable nerve damage.

Answering an advert in a gay magazine, Justin met his first long-term partner, who lived in Southampton. Justin got a job as an auxiliary nurse, a job which he loved, and with a steady relationship, life became more settled. Some years later, Justin returned home after work and found his partner entertaining other men. The relationship fell apart. Justin left Southampton and moved to Bournemouth, but soon his health began to deteriorate and, because he was unable to lift, he lost his job as a nurse. Promised another job within the NHS, he went to 12 job interviews but without success. With life spiralling downhill, Justin took to alcohol and was an alcoholic for seven years. Through his alcohol abuse, he lost his home and moved back to Southampton to stay with a friend. It was then that he signed on to my list.

The more Justin recounted the sadness of his life, the more I began to 'feel with' him and I realised that there was a very real reason for his problems. Towards the end of the conversation I said to Justin; 'Have you ever thought about coming to church?' 'Oh I used to go to church' he replied. 'I went along to an evangelical church and got really involved; I wrote hymns and I even helped the minister write his sermons. Then they found out I was gay, and they threw me out: I have never been back.' When Justin said this I was ashamed. As Christians we had heaped even more condemnation upon this man, offering him neither acceptance, love, nor mercy.

Deflated, I felt I had nothing more to offer Justin and he got up and left. Leaving my room Justin left the door ajar. As he walked out into the waiting room, a lovely Irish lady waiting for her appointment saw him and jumped up from her chair. She said to Justin 'Hello beautiful,' planting a great big kiss on his cheek. Then turning to the person next to her she said: 'Isn't he the most handsome of men?' And I felt God whisper to me; 'Now *that's* grace.'

My rather condescending and smug attitude towards Justin had been revealed by God for what it was. In the midst of all Justin's problems, his alcohol and medical illness, his homosexuality, his lifestyle, I had looked for a *reason* to love him. I felt more inclined to extend an arm of mercy to Justin when I could understand why he was the way he was. My Irish patient in the waiting room needed no reason to love Justin. In her eyes he was just 'beautiful', and 'the most handsome of men.'

I have come to understand now that God's grace, his love, and his heart of compassion, do not seek a reason to be offered. God simply sees each one of us as beautiful, the most handsome of men, the most beautiful of women, and he simply loves us for who we are. Philip Yancey writes:

A prostitute, a wealthy exploiter, a demon-possessed woman, a Roman soldier, a Samaritan with running sores and another Samaritan with serial husbands – I marvel that Jesus gained the reputation as being a 'friend of sinners' like these. As Helmut Thielicke wrote: 'Jesus gained the power to love harlots, bullies and ruffians ... he was able to do this because he saw through the filth and crust of degeneration, because his eye caught the divine original which is hidden in every way – in every man! ... First and foremost he gives us new eyes ... When Jesus loved a guilt-laden person and helped him, he saw in him an erring child of God. He saw in him a human being whom his father loved and grieved over because he was going wrong. He saw him as God originally designed and meant him to be, and therefore he saw through the surface layer of grime and dirt to the real man underneath. Jesus did not identify *the person with his sin, but rather saw in this sin something alien, something that really did not belong to him, something that merely chained and mastered him and from which he would free him and bring him back to his real self. Jesus was able to love men because he loved them right through the layer of mud.'*

We may be abominations but we are still God's pride and joy. All of us in the church need 'grace-healed eyes' to see the potential in others for the same grace that God so lavishly bestowed on us. 'To love a person,' said Dostoevsky, 'means to see him as God intended him to be.'[2]

My wife Sheelagh has captured something of this divine perspective: her password on the computer is 'gorgeous'. Now to those who don't know her, this may seem arrogant and presumptuous. Those of us who do know her, know that not only is this true, but that Sheelagh is simply accepting what God feels about her. He sees us all in the same light. He sees right through the layers of filth, to the gorgeous and unique people that we are.

One Saturday evening some years ago, my youngest daughter, Deborah, then aged twelve, found herself alone with us at home. Sensing this was her opportunity to finally get first choice at TV viewing, she asked Sheelagh if we could get a video out and watch it together. Sheelagh readily agreed and she and Deborah went down to the local video store to get a film of Deborah's choosing. I had to say that this left me feeling a little anxious because, knowing Sheelagh and Deborah's choice of movie entertainment, I was expecting a girly film or *The Sound of Music*. When they arrived back at home, my worst fears were realised – *Patch Adams*. (I hadn't got a clue what the film was about, having only heard of the title, but one look at the cover revealed that there weren't going to be too many car chases.) So we sat down together to watch it. I was less than enthusiastic, expecting to find the film rather tedious, but I was soon to realise how wrong I was.

Patch Adams is a film based on a true story of a man who enters medical school as a mature student and becomes a rather unorthodox doctor. Throughout the film, pictures of grace punctuate the story. One particular sequence, however, stood out, and taught me another important lesson.

Hunter Adams, played in the film by Robin Williams, has a mental breakdown and is admitted to the Fairfax Hospital. The opening scene details his hospital admission – a forlorn and depressed figure entering the lonely and frightening world of a psychiatric ward. On entering the ward, he is rather dramatically confronted by an old man who thrusts four fingers in his face and aggressively asks how many fingers he sees. Taken aback, Hunter answers 'Four.' 'Four? Four? Hmm, another idiot!' the old man replies.

The man was apparently mad. The Nurse explains that he is Arthur Mendelson, a well known genius who has clearly gone out of his mind. During Hunter's time in the hospital, Arthur is seen asking the same question of other patients. On receiving the same reply, he goes off in disgust saying, 'You're all insane!'

Hunter settles on the ward and finds he has a gift of helping others, through his humour and non-conformity. By contrast, the ward doctor is presented as a man simply going through the motions of providing medical care; when Hunter is 'clerked' in as a patient, the doctor is more concerned about sorting out his coffee, than listening to what Hunter has to say.

Following his encounter with the genius Arthur Mendelson, Hunter is intrigued by the 'four fingers', and so goes to Arthur's room to confront him. He encounters a gruff, unapproachable figure, hunched at his desk, poring over impossible mathematical formulas. Unperturbed by the cold reception, Hunter questions Arthur:

> *'The fingers, what's the answer?'*
> *'Young fellows who always know the right answer. Welcome to the real world.'*

The old man mumbles without even looking up from his formulas. Sitting in silence, Hunter notices Arthur's disposable coffee cup is leaking, and patches it up with a piece of sticky tape. Attracted by this tiny act of kindness, Arthur is drawn away from his formulas and turns to face Hunter. Taking Hunter's hand in his own, he forms four fingers on Hunter's hand and holds them up between their two faces.

> *'How many do you see?'*
> *'There are four fingers, Arthur.'*
> *'No, no, no! Look at me!'*
> *'What?'*
> *'You're focusing on the problem. If you focus on the problem, you can't see the solution. Never focus on the problem; look at me! Now, how many do you see?'*

Hunter focuses his eyes on his fingers again and Arthur again tells him to look beyond them.

As Hunter re-focuses his eyes on Arthur's face, the fingers blur, and he sees not four fingers, but eight. Hunter timidly responds:

> *'Eight.'*
> *'Eight, eight! Yes, yes, eight's a good answer. See what no-one else sees; see what everyone else chooses not to see, out of fear or conformity or laziness. See the whole world anew each day'* ...
>
> *Stunned, Hunter says: 'What do you see in me, Arthur?'*
>
> *Arthur replies: 'You fixed my cup. I'll see you around ... Patch!'*[3]

> *Hunter takes on his new name and, on recovering from his mental breakdown, embarks upon his medical training. He learns to 'see people as no-one else sees them', treating patients as real people and not simply as interesting medical cases. His unorthodox methods of care and his zany humour lead him to confrontation with the medical establishment, but his compassion finally wins them over. Throughout his student days, Hunter pursues the affection of an attractive young woman, Carin Fisher, who has herself been the subject of abuse by men. In a tragic and poignant twist, Carin loses her life at the hands of one of Patch's mentally disturbed friends. Having warned Patch of the threat she felt this patient posed, Patch could barely come to terms with his grief. However, through his sadness, we are reminded of something he had once said to Carin:*

> *'If we don't show him compassion, who will?'*

These words, almost spiritual in their resonance, remind us that Patch's life was devoted to seeing everyone through grace-filled eyes, regardless. As the film ends, we are told that, following his qualification as a doctor, 'Patch' Adams opened a family-based medical centre, treating over fifteen thousand patients without charge.

I realise now that I had viewed Justin with the wrong eyes. I had been looking at the 'fingers': his medical problems, his alcohol abuse, his sexual orientation. By focusing my attention on his problems, I had failed to look at *him*. When the God of grace looks upon his children, he sees through the 'layer of grime and mud' and sees the person he intended when he first made us. He sees the beauty, the potential, and the value that we are in his eyes. If we are to lead grace-filled lives we need to look through the 'fingers' of another person's life, through the dirt and the grime, and see the person made in the image of God.

In chapter 2, I referred to the narrow road that we walk as Christians, the road which is our daily walk in Christ. Off the road to one side are the dangers of Pharisaism and legalism and on the other side are the dangers of liberalism and licence. I see the boundaries of the road, as being the boundaries of grace and truth. By erring too far on the side of truth there is the danger of falling into legalism, and by erring too far on the side of grace there is the danger of falling into licence. This can lead to a tension within the Christian life and often makes following our faith difficult. In truth, I believe that abortion is wrong and grieves the heart of God, and yet by grace I know that God loves every woman who faces an unplanned pregnancy, even if they continue with their plans to abort their child. The actions of those who burn down abortion clinics, or even worse, shoot and kill doctors who perform abortions, are to me the actions of those who have erred too far on the side of truth. They believe their actions are justified through defending the 'truth' that abortion is morally wrong, and yet they have failed to understand the grace of God which extends his hand of compassion to those lives that have been destroyed through sin.

When the woman was brought to Jesus, caught in the very act of adultery, his act of mercy towards her did not condone her sin. But his reaction to her sin was not one of judgement. By extending his hand of love towards her, by not condemning her, he was able to point her in a new direction: 'Go and sin no more' (Jn. 8:11). It has often been said that 'God hates the sin, but loves the sinner.' The pathway of grace and truth is exactly this, and although it is a difficult and narrow road, it is made possible by the One who has gone before.

In John's gospel chapter 1, we read: 'And the word became flesh, and dwelt amongst us, *full of grace and truth*' (my emphasis). In Jesus we see this perfect harmony of grace and truth in all its fullness. As we commit to a life centred on Jesus, we have access to this pathway which is grace and truth. As we are confronted by the seeming impossibilities of broken lives – whether in the pregnancy crisis centre, the surgery, our office, or our neighbourhood – we cannot rely on yesterday's experiences as a solution for today's challenges. Every individual person presents a unique life which demands an equally unique response of God's grace and truth. We now come back to the discipline of the compassionate lifestyle, by which we are able to live a life full of grace and truth, asking God daily to guide us and teach us.

There are many issues that challenge the Christian church today and abortion is just one of them. At the present time within the Church of England the issue of homosexuality is causing great division. In his book *Abba's Child*, Brennan Manning states:

> Homophobia ranks as one of the most shameful scandals of my life time. In this closing decade of the twentieth century, it is frightening to see the intolerance, moral absolutism and unbending dogmatism that prevail when people insist upon taking the religious high ground. Alan Jones noted that 'It is precisely among those who take their spiritual lifestyle seriously that the greatest danger lies.' Pious people are as easily victimised by the tyranny of homophobia as anyone else.[4]

Philip Yancey describes this homophobic attitude graphically after investigating the issue more deeply through the influence of his homosexual friend, Mel White.

> Every gay person I interviewed could tell hair-raising tales of rejection, hatred, and persecution, most have been called names and beaten up too many times to count. Half the

people I interviewed had been disowned by their families ... Some Christians say, 'Yes we should treat gays with compassion but at the same time we must give them the message of judgement.' After all these interviews, I began to understand that every gay person has heard the message of judgement from the church – again and again, nothing but judgement ...

I started making it a point to meet other gay people in our neighbourhood including some who came from a Christian background. 'I still believe,' one told me, 'I would love to go to church, but whenever I've tried someone spreads a rumor about me and suddenly everybody withdraws.' He added a chilling remark, 'As a gay man, I found it easier for me to get sex on the streets than to get a hug in church.'[5]

For my patient, Justin, the experience was the same. Looking for love and acceptance within an evangelical community he found rejection and was ostracised as soon as his homosexuality came to light. As Brennan Manning says, 'the number of people who have fled the church because it is too patient or compassionate is negligible; the number who have fled because they have found it too unforgiving is tragic.'[6] Whether we face a woman requesting abortion, a homosexual colleague, a drug addict on the street, or a teenage car thief, we must look through 'the fingers' and see the beautiful image that God intended. We cannot *grade* their sin according to our own morals and lifestyles. It seems to me that the Bible does not grade sin at all; indeed, Paul writes in the book of Romans, 'for all have sinned and fallen short of the glory of God' (3:23). We have *all* missed the mark. We cannot claim to be less sinful than others: there are no 'near misses' with God, we have all simply missed it. The broken and sinful lives of others should disgust us no more than our own sinful brokenness. By grace God has rescued us from our own rottenness and, in a daily walk of gratitude, we should extend that same measure of grace to all around us.

> *But even though we were dead in our sins God, who is rich in mercy, because of the great love he had for us, gave us life together with Christ – it is, remember, by grace and not by achievement that you are saved – and has lifted us right out of the old life to take our place with him in Christ Jesus in the Heaven. Thus he shows for all time the tremendous generosity of the grace and kindness he has expressed towards us in Christ Jesus. It was nothing you could or did achieve – it was God's gift of grace which saved you. No one can pride himself upon earning the love of God. The fact is that what we are we owe to the hand of God upon us.*

> *Ephesians 2:5–10, J. B. Phillips*

Your Grace

Unjustified
Undignified
to put aside
my lifetime's sin
and encase within
Your perfect love
Your grace
That finds infinite beauty
In shattered shards
Of my life
And transforms brokenness
Into reflected radiance
Of Your Glory

Rebekah Clarke

The Joy in Loving

He who is kind to the poor lends to the Lord, and he will repay him for his deeds.

Proverbs 19:17

One of the most remarkable lives given in the service of others was that of Mother Teresa of Calcutta. The title of this chapter is sourced from the book of the same name, a collection of thoughts by Mother Teresa, compiled and laid out as an aid to daily devotion. Mother Teresa of Calcutta was born Agnes Bojaxhiu in the city of Skopje (now in the former Yugoslav Republic of Macedonia), in 1910. Her parents were Albanian and she was the youngest of three children. At a very young age, she felt called to a life of religious service and joined a Catholic youth group in her home town of Skopje. At the age of eighteen, Agnes moved to Ireland to join the Sisters of our Lady of Loreto. In the following year she experienced her first taste of life in Calcutta, India, but it was not until many years later, in 1948, that she returned there. Agnes' unerring commitment to Calcutta would become one of the most defining features of the city's social history.

Before moving to Calcutta, Agnes continued her training in the northern Indian state of Darjeeling, at a convent run by the Sisters of our Lady of Loreto. From here, she was sent to Loreto Entally, one of six schools

run by the Sisters in Calcutta. It was on a train journey
to Darjeeling that she became 'aware of a calling in the
midst of my vocation: I had to leave the convent and go
to Loreto Entally and consecrate myself to help the poor,
living among them.' So began the work of Mother Teresa,
amongst the poorest of the poor in the city of Calcutta. At
that time, the city of Calcutta had three thousand official
slums with over two million starving and destitute people.
Many of these people had no homes but struggled to
survive on street pavements and in railway stations. It was
to these people that Mother Teresa devoted her life. She
sacrificed everything, denying herself, her own comforts,
personal wealth and possessions, and giving all she had
to those who were in such desperate need.

The philosophy that Mother Teresa instilled in the Sisters
in her 'Missionaries of Charity' was that as they served the
poor and destitute on the street of Calcutta, they should see
in each of them the person of Christ. In giving their love
and kindness to that person they were, in fact, bestowing
that kindness on Christ himself. They came to realise that
Christ would come to them in the guise of the hungry, in
the guise of the leper, in the guise of an alcoholic, in the
guise of the terminally ill and in the guise of the lonely and
abandoned. Whoever God brought to her or her missionary
sisters, they treated with the utmost dignity and respect,
recognising that in their acts of mercy they were attending
to the Lord Himself. Mother Teresa once said:

> *Today the Poor are hungry for bread and rice – and for love and*
> *the living word of God; the Poor are thirsty – for water and for*
> *peace, truth and justice; the Poor are naked – for clothes, for*
> *human dignity and compassion for the naked sinner.*
>
> *The Poor are homeless – for a shelter made of bricks and for a*
> *joyful heart that understands, covers, loves. They are sick – for*
> *medical care – and for that gentle touch and a warm smile.*

The 'shut in', the unwanted, the unloved, the alcoholics, the dying destitutes, the abandoned and the lonely, the outcasts and the untouchables, the leprosy sufferers – all those who are a burden to the human society – who have lost all hope and faith in life – who have forgotten how to smile – who have lost the sensibility of the warm hand touch of love and friendship – they look to us for comfort – if we turn our back on them, we turn it on Christ, and at the hour of our death we will be judged if we have recognised Christ in them, and what we have done for and to them.[1]

The ability of Mother Teresa to see Christ in the 'poorest of the poor' is a quality that we should all aspire to learn. In his book, *Ruthless Trust*, Brennan Manning tells the story of a meeting he had with Dorothy Day, the seventy-three-year-old founder of the Catholic Worker Movement. He had met her on Christmas Eve, after helping the workers tend to the hungry and homeless. Dorothy asks:

'Brennan, I'm sure you are familiar with Peter Claver.'

'Yes, ma'am,' I replied. 'Back in the 1640s he had a ministry to blacks who had been commandeered into the slave trade, often beaten to a pulp and left for dead. Claver burned out his short life, like a modern-day paramedic, alleviating their suffering or providing them care and spiritual comfort when they died.'

This wizened old woman who cried the Gospel with her life said, 'One night Peter recruited a couple of volunteers to help minister to a dying man whose suppurating flesh had been eaten away because of years in chains. When the volunteers saw the oozing flesh and smelled the putrid odour, they ran panic-stricken from the room. Peter cried out, 'You mustn't go. You can't leave him – it is Christ.'[2]

In the Sermon on the Mount Jesus says 'Blessed are the merciful, for they shall obtain mercy' (Mt. 5:7) and the word blessed can be translated here as: 'How happy' are the merciful. One of the challenges currently facing Christians in Western society is learning to focus our eyes on matters of the heart. Living amongst the fast-paced and often commodity-driven culture of the twenty-first century it is easy to become swept up in the value of material possessions and shallow quick-fix solutions. Our value, and the value we find in others, should be inspired and found in Jesus, and the example he displayed in the gospels. Christ's teachings turned the world's values on their head, and the life of Mother Teresa is a sparkling example of a person finding true happiness in total givenness. Not only did she find joy in her own life but she inspired joy and happiness in others too.

Mother Teresa tells this story:

> *One night, a man came to our house to tell me that a Hindu family, a family of eight children, had not eaten anything for days. They had nothing to eat. I took enough rice for a meal and went to their house. I could see the hungry faces, the children with their bulging eyes. The sight could not have been more dramatic! The mother took the rice from my hands, divided it in half and went out. When she came back a little later, I asked her: 'Where did you go? What did you do?' She answered, 'They also are hungry.' 'They' were the people next door, a Muslim family with the same number of children to feed and who did not have any food either. That mother was aware of the situation. She had the courage and the love to share her meager portion of rice with others. In spite of her circumstances, I think she felt very happy to share with her neighbors the little I had taken her. In order not to take away her happiness, I did not take her any more rice that night. I took her some more the following day.*[3]

So often we find that those who have very little are often the most generous givers. In Mark's gospel, Jesus commends the poor widow who gave 'everything she had, her whole living' (12:42). In our own society we can so easily fall victim to always wanting more. Although we should celebrate living in the society in which God has placed us, we need to learn to hold our money and possessions lightly, to make them available to God. If he prompts us to give to those who are less fortunate, we should not find this a burden, but simply a joy. We may not have the slums of Calcutta and the incredible destitution that confronted Mother Teresa and her Sisters, but poverty is all around us. We often think of poverty simply in terms of having no money and no possessions, but if we assume such a narrow view of poverty, we sometimes miss identifying the needs of people all around us. The Missionary of Charity have established communities all around the world, including in the West, and have helped us to understand that poverty exists everywhere. Mother Teresa wrote:

> *One night in London I went out visiting people with the Sisters. We saw a boy with long hair, sitting in the street with others. I spoke to him and said: 'You shouldn't be here, you should be with your mother and father, this is not the place for you.' The young boy said: 'My mother does not want me. Each time I go home, she pushes me out, because she can't bear my long hair.' We passed on. When I came back he was lying flat on the ground. He had overdosed himself. We had to take him to hospital. I could not help but reflect: here was a child hungry for home, and his mother had no time for him. This is great poverty. This is where you and I must make this world a better world.*[4]

Some years ago, I attended a very elderly couple, both in their nineties, who were very rich, having been in business all of their working lives. They had no children, were obsessed with their health, lived very reclusive lives, had few friends and were very lonely. Despite their wealth they lived in enormous 'poverty' and as the end of their lives approached they were both very frightened and lonely. I was able to share my faith with both of them and, before their deaths, prayed with both of them in true simplicity of faith. I believe that both of them in their last few days of life found hope in a living Saviour. Whether we live in Calcutta or Southampton, the 'poor' are all around us; the lonely pensioner next door, the young mother struggling to cope alone with her children, the alcoholics, the child who has been bullied at school, the young woman facing an unexpected pregnancy. The opportunities to reach out and love those who are 'poor' are simply endless.

The joy and blessing that comes from loving other people is not a smug self-satisfaction, a 'holier than thou' attitude, or the false piety of a perceived holiness. The joy stems from recognising that, as we give ourselves to others and see in them 'Christ in the guise of the poor', we ourselves simply draw closer to God. We are reminded of our own 'poverty' and discover afresh the hand of God's blessing on our own lives. In the book of Isaiah, God's people questioned why the Lord was apparently not hearing their prayers, and not blessing them. They displayed their piety in fasting and prayer and yet God rebuked them because, despite all their devotions, they had failed to consider the needs of the poor. God's blessings were withheld, their joy was lacking, and they could not find closeness with God.

This is the kind of fast day I am after; to break the chains of injustice, get rid of exploitation in the work place, free the oppressed, cancel debt. What I am interested in seeing you do is: sharing your food with the hungry, inviting the homeless poor into your homes, putting clothes on the shivering ill-clad, being available to your own families. Do this and the lights will turn on, and your lives will turn around at once. Your righteousness will pave your way. The GOD *of glory will secure your passage when you pray. Then* GOD *will answer. You will call out for help and I will say 'here I am'.*

Isaiah 58:6–8, The Message

The full joy in loving comes from a closer relationship with God. Sometimes we discover that God graciously answers our prayers as we draw close to him through loving others. At the outset of the development of the work of Firgrove, we met as a steering group each month and set goals and plans to be achieved by the next meeting. What astounded us all was that it seemed that almost before we had finished praying about our goals for the month, God had not only answered them but provided even more than we had expected. Our experiences in Firgrove, and since then in Care Centres Network, have not been of waiting around in the hope that God will do something, but of us running after him trying desperately to keep up with what he wants us to do. God's heart for the poor is so big, that we only need to make ourselves available to respond to the need he calls us to, and we find closeness with him that we may never have experienced before. During my time with the Community Church I have been part of many church activities, but through the work of Firgrove and Care Centres Network, I have experienced more miraculous working and learned more about the heart of God than in all my previous experiences put together. Of course, this is not to say that other church activities are less important. At the time of my involvement in the other areas of service I had not understood the importance that God places on a life which is given to the service of those who are in need. The Firgrove work and the work of Care Centres Network has opened my eyes to the enormous compassion God has for every person in society and the desire that he has for us as Christians, in whatever role we have in the church, to reach out in love, mercy and kindness, to those who are in any respect poor.

In August of 2003 I turned fifty. Often these milestones are times when we can reflect on our lives, on what has been achieved and what our priorities are, and on our hopes for the future. Reflecting on my life, the chief moments of joy and happiness are all centred on relationships and people, not possessions and things. As a child, my joyful memories were not of when my father bought a new car, but of the times we spent together at Christmas with my extended family, of going on holiday together and of sharing life. As I look back on the 28 years of my marriage, all of our joy and happiness has stemmed from our loving relationships and times spent together rather than the possessions that we have accumulated. I can still hear the screams of delight from my daughter Rebekah when we announced to the children that we were going on holiday to the United States. I can still see the joy on the face of my son James, as we rode the biggest roller-coasters together at Knotts' Berry Farm. I still see the wonder in Deborah's eyes, gazing at the light parade in Disneyland. I still picture Catherine bringing the sun-bleached bones of a dead animal from the hillsides high above Death Valley, asking could she take them home.

Similarly, in our work in medicine or through the centres, as we have learned to give and share with others, we have had many incredibly joyful experiences, which have all led to a deeper understanding of the heart of God and a closer walk with him. When I was a young Houseman working on a surgical ward in Southampton a severely physically disabled man in his early forties was admitted for a simple hernia repair operation. Despite the relatively minor nature of this surgery, because of Paddy's disability, we planned to keep him in hospital for a number of days. Paddy 'lived' in an institution on the outskirts of Southampton, which at the time could best be described as exceedingly grim. The old run-down hospital which he knew as home housed a number of physically handicapped people. But more than this, it was home to the most severely mentally handicapped and brain-damaged people within our society. Paddy, himself had very severe cerebral palsy and presented a twisted and broken picture of humanity. He was unable to attend to his own personal needs, his speech was slurred and at times difficult to comprehend and yet this man was far from unintelligent. Indeed, some years earlier he had studied for a science O level and having had special dispensation from the examining board, giving him time to convey his knowledge, he had passed with flying colours.

Paddy's operation was scheduled for early in the week, but he was admitted several days beforehand so that we could run a series of tests and investigations, and ensure his safety throughout the surgery. As a Junior Houseman I had the responsibility to 'clerk' him in, taking all the details of his history, examining him, and initiating his investigations. The sorrow in Paddy's eyes as he recounted his life in the institution was clearly evident and I felt very sad that society had abandoned an intelligent but physically broken man.

Unusually, neither Sheelagh nor I were working the weekend prior to Paddy's surgery, so we decided to go up to the hospital and take Paddy out in his wheelchair into Southampton to look around the shops. The experience was like taking a child to Disneyland. The sadness in Paddy's eyes disappeared and a simple shopping trip down the high street of Southampton filled him with more joy than I have seen in anybody. We bought him a new cardigan in a style that he had always wanted, and his beaming smile as he presented himself to the nurses back on the ward was a sight to behold. The following week Paddy's surgery went ahead without any problems and within a few days he was ready to be discharged.

As the day of his discharge neared, Paddy seemed to become less outgoing and when the ambulance men arrived to transfer him back to his 'home' he burst into tears. 'Do I have to go home? I am so happy here,' he pleaded. I found it heartbreaking that any human being could be 'happy' on a surgical ward in a Southampton hospital.

Paddy's plight had touched me profoundly and at our house group a number of my friends agreed to visit Paddy and see if together we could bring back the joy of those brief days in hospital. Steve and Maresah Haines and Angela Barr were not only able to see Paddy, but also bring him along to church and to other events. Unfortunately my work prevented me from being heavily involved in this, but the willingness of my friends to give their time and love was wonderful. Despite my arduous on-call responsibilities I would see Paddy on a regular basis and his joy and happiness in being amongst us was infectious. Because of his disabilities, when he laughed, he sounded more like a sea lion, but this only led to even greater hilarity amongst us and the times we had together were such fun.

It was not long before Paddy gave his life to God and despite his disability he was baptised in the church. A few months later (and to this day I do not understand how) Paddy was transferred from the institution he had lived for the previous eighteen years, to a Christian care home, purpose-built, on the outskirts of Bournemouth. I was only able to visit Paddy once in the short time that he spent in Bournemouth before he died, but during that time he became involved in a church and lived out a radiant life to the glory of God. I will never forget Paddy, his infectious sea lion laugh, and the joy that he radiated out to those around about him. Such is the joy of loving.

In Kathryn Spink's authorised biography of Mother Teresa, she tells the story of a worker who helped on a voluntary basis in Shishu Bhavan, the children's home established by Mother Teresa in Calcutta:

She would go from one tiny baby to the next, and if she spotted one that was so frail or sick that it seemed likely to die that day, she would wrap it in a blanket and give it to one of the helpers to hold, with the instruction simply to love that child until it died. What mattered was that no child in her care would die without having experienced love. One morning Mother Teresa placed one of these desperately sick babies in the arms of one of the lay helpers. The helper held it and loved it until it finally died at 6 o'clock in the evening. She passed away the hours by humming Brahms' lullaby. More than thirty years later she would still retain the memory of how that tiny baby, weak as it was, pressed itself against her.[5]

A few years ago a woman in her late thirties came in to the Firgrove Centre. She had missed several periods, and felt that she might be pregnant, so requested a pregnancy test. However, her pregnancy seemed impossible. Both she and her husband were professional people and had decided not to have a family. Such was their determination to remain childless and pursue their careers, that he had had a vasectomy. Three years following the operation, he had his sperm count checked, to ensure that there was absolutely no chance of his wife conceiving. However, when Sheelagh did a pregnancy test she found that, to her amazement, Sophie was pregnant. She was concerned at having to break this devastating news to her. The decision that Sophie and her husband had made never to have children meant that an abortion was the only option. Sophie was distraught, and Sheelagh felt that she had little opportunity to affect her intended course of action. She nevertheless spent a considerable amount of time just being with Sophie in her time of need, carefully explaining to her the options that were open to her and supporting her in whatever decision she made.

Sophie left the Firgrove Centre in a state of considerable distress and Sheelagh was left with the distinct impression that there would be no doubt that she would proceed with a termination of pregnancy. It was a great surprise, therefore, that she received a letter from Sophie at the end of the following week.

Dear Sheelagh,

Do you remember me? I came to visit you last Saturday 7th at 10.00am. Piedad [one of our other advisors at the Centre] arranged and helped me with that. Kindly thank her. Before I go on just let me apologise for this terrible paper. I am at work and thinking how kind you were – so decided to drop you a line now. I wanted to basically say a huge thank you to you. I found just talking to you along with listening to your advice was invaluable. As soon as I left the Firgrove Centre I ran across to Butlers Bakery and bought the biggest jam doughnut there was to console myself. I then went home to my lovely hubby, who just like me was in shock for three days. To begin with the decision was a very definite abortion. Then the next day – over the shock, thinking about it [*sic*].

We actually made this terribly important decision yesterday. We are looking forward to having our baby at Easter. I just want to say thank you again. I listened to you, you were a tremendous help.

With kindest regards,
Sophie

PS I will *never* forget the moment you walked into the room and said 'Sophie I am afraid the test is positive.' We are framing the confirmation slip that you gave us.

Incredibly, Sophie's pregnancy was the result of the failure of her husband's vasectomy and, despite the operation being performed many years earlier, his body had spontaneously and naturally reversed the procedure. Not only did Sheelagh have the joy of being involved in the early life of Sophie's unborn baby, but her joy was multiplied when after the birth Sophie rang Sheelagh to ask her to be her baby's godmother.

The joy of experiencing a mother choosing life for her unborn child is multiplied as we pray for that little life, asking God to fulfil all his dreams and plans in that child as he or she grows. Joanna Thompson tells a remarkable story revealing that God has been answering those prayers.

Suzanne's Story

Suzanne came with her boyfriend to a local pregnancy crisis centre that had recently opened. They were both very young, frightened and were shocked at the positive result to a pregnancy test. They even thought of running away to avoid telling Suzanne's parents but realised this would solve nothing. Together with their counsellor, Joanna, they looked at the various options open to them. They were both particularly struck by the leaflet on the development of the baby.

They came back to the centre three times but even after the last visit Joanna still didn't know what they would choose to do. However she asked the rest of the team to join her in praying for Suzanne, her boyfriend and their baby. They heard no more but Joanna found it hard to forget Suzanne.

About ten years later Joanna was taking a seminar at Stoneleigh Bible Week explaining how our role is to love, care and support women coming for help, offering them the opportunity to look at all the facts and explore their options so they can make their own informed decision; that we rely on the Holy Spirit to show women what is the right thing to do. A woman in the front row stood up and said, 'That's what happened to me. I came to your centre and you showed me that I had a choice. I couldn't get over the fact that my baby already had fingernails.' She went on to say that she had decided to keep her baby. He was now eleven and was at Stoneleigh with her.

After the meeting, Suzanne told Joanna that ever since her son could talk, he had talked to Jesus, and then a little later would draw pictures for him and write little notes to him. Because of this Suzanne had decided to take her son to Sunday school. It was through this Sunday school that Suzanne also learned about the love of God and she became a Christian. Joanna was reminded how, when the centres first began, we had felt encouraged to pray for every child that was born as a result of their mother coming to a centre. She told Suzanne, 'We prayed that God would not only save these little ones' lives but that he will also touch them spiritually.'

After the seminar Joanna kept in touch with Suzanne and continued to pray for them as a family. It was with great joy that she accepted an invitation to her wedding. David, her partner, had also just become a Christian, been baptised and now they wanted to marry. Their son, now aged thirteen was their best man.

Some years ago, Sheelagh and I and three other counsellors from Firgrove travelled to South Africa. We were invited to help with some training to set up pregnancy counselling centres across the country. With the overthrow of the apartheid regime, the incoming government had reformed the laws on abortion, making abortion legal in South Africa and available to all. The church in South Africa recognised their need to establish a network of support in response to this change in the Law. We felt privileged to be involved in helping the development of South Africa Cares for Life in a tiny way. At the forefront of this work is a lady called Riekie Van De Berg. Riekie is a social worker who lives in Pretoria and is a wonderfully gracious woman of God. Since our meeting with Riekie many years ago, our own national co-ordinator, Joanna Thompson, has been able to travel to South Africa on many occasions and in turn Riekie has been able to visit us here in England. During Joanna's most recent trip to South Africa, she and Riekie were involved in a most amazing work of God.

One morning Riekie and Joanna were due to visit a pregnancy crisis centre in a rural area where there was great poverty. Because of the immense neediness of the area, the work of the centre had diversified and much of the time was spent helping and counselling women who were HIV positive. A clinic was also involved with a programme providing food for the poorest families, paying particular attention to those families where there were absent fathers.

On the morning of the proposed trip, Riekie felt very unwell, but she insisted on going to the centre with Joanna. It was as though she felt compelled to go. That day, they aimed to visit four out of twenty families who were on the list in need of urgent food supplies. As they entered the first home, they were met by an elderly lady, Granny Gogo, who was caring for five of her grandchildren. They lived in two rooms; four of the grandmother's own children had died of AIDS during the last year including the mother of the five children that she was caring for. The youngest of these children, baby Lydia, was no bigger than a newborn baby. She was obviously very sick and undernourished. Granny Gogo was doing her very best for the children in the midst of dreadful suffering but it was clear that Lydia was critically ill. In her role as a social worker, Riekie decided that she would ask to take baby Lydia into the care of one of her nurseries that she had set up through the work of South Africa Cares for Life. Granny Gogo was relieved because the baby had not eaten for two days and had been crying continuously for the previous two weeks. No one in the family had slept and the baby's uncle cried tears of relief as Riekie brought hope and resolution to their impossible situation.

Riekie planned to keep baby Lydia with them while they visited the other families in need, but Joanna insisted on seeking immediate medical advice because Lydia looked so unwell. Amazingly, they were able to get an appointment with the doctor later that day. As soon as the doctor saw Lydia she wanted to admit her immediately to hospital, but said that Lydia would probably not survive the journey because she was so dehydrated. The doctor immediately set up an intravenous infusion and within minutes Lydia began to respond to the medical help. Riekie and Joanna were then able to take Lydia to the hospital where she received more intensive care.

Returning home to the UK, Joanna felt that it had been a privilege to be involved with rescuing baby Lydia from a certain death. Joanna was, therefore, surprised and a little discouraged when Riekie contacted her from South Africa and said that although Lydia had been discharged back into her care at Abba Nurseries, she had recently taken a turn for the worse and had again become very weak. That night Joanna had a strange dream about dying – rather than being frightening, however, the death depicted in her dream was very peaceful. Awaking abruptly from the dream, Joanna found that Lydia immediately came to her mind, and so she started to pray for her. Joanna sensed that Lydia was dying and yet it seemed so strange that this should be the case since she felt that God had intervened and saved her from death only weeks earlier.

The next morning Joanna received an e-mail from Riekie to say that Lydia had died in the night. Although Joanna was really upset, she felt somehow that God was in control. But what was God doing? Why should they have rescued Lydia from her grandmother if she was going to die anyway? Riekie wrote to say that they had paid for the funeral for Lydia and then invited the grandmother and her other grandchildren to their annual Christmas party. Joanna felt that she should write Granny Gogo a letter. Joanna herself has grandchildren, and so from one grandmother to another, she wanted to simply express her love and compassion for her. This was Joanna's letter:

Dear Gogo,
I am hoping that my friend Riekie will read this letter to you. I came to your house with Riekie this

summer, the day that your little granddaughter left
with us to receive medical care. My heart so went
out to you. I too, am a grandmother and I could
only imagine what it must have been like to see your
granddaughter so poorly.

I was extremely sorry to hear that little Lydia had
died. I have been praying for her and asking Jesus
to watch over her. I do believe that she is now safe
with him. I knew that she had been getting weaker.
One night I woke in the middle of the night after
having a dream about dying. It was not frightening
at all but very peaceful. I asked Jesus what it was
all about and your little granddaughter came to
mind, so I prayed and prayed for her. I felt that
she was quietly slipping into heaven and that Jesus
was there holding her hand. The very next morning
Riekie wrote to me to say that in the night Lydia
had died. I do hope this brings you a little comfort.
It is so hard to understand these things, and I don't
begin to. But I do believe that Jesus loves your little
Lydia very much and that he came for her and that
now she is with him in peace.

Since returning to the United Kingdom where
I live, you have often been on my heart. I wonder
how you are managing caring for your other
grandchildren. I do pray for you that God will
give you courage and strength to care for them.
It was so obvious to me how much you love them
and how well you try and look after them with so
few resources. You have my deepest respect. I have
arranged for a small amount of money [*The money
was donated from people in the UK with whom Joanna
had shared the story*] to be paid to Riekie and have

asked her to use this to help you in whatever way she thinks best. Please receive it with my love – from one grandmother to another.

I will continue to pray for you and your grandchildren. I do not know why God arranged for me to meet you or why he has put you so much on my heart. I can only imagine it is because he has seen your life, your pain, grief and your determination to care for your family and his heart is filled with love and compassion for you. I pray that as Riekie reads this to you, the presence of Jesus will be very real and that you will come to know him as your friend and Saviour just as I did some years ago.

I do hope that you will allow me to write to you again and that Riekie can pass on news to me of how you are managing.

With love in Jesus,
Joanna

At the Christmas party Riekie read Joanna's letter to Lydia's grandmother. Apparently, years ago she had invited Jesus into her life but she had had little real understanding of what that meant. When AIDS had started to kill her family, something started to die in her heart, and she began to lose her faith. Later Riekie wrote Joanna an e-mail.

I visited Gogo and her family just before I left for the Christmas holidays, and it was an amazing day. Gogo welcomed me as if I was an angel. When we arrived there she was busy doing Bible study and she started to pray for us and thanked Jesus for everything we are doing for them. Then she told me how she prayed since her first daughter died (from AIDS) and asked Jesus to save them from this terrible disease. She shared how she almost lost faith when her other children died and when she realised that Lydia was also sick and dying. She told me that she prayed, saying that if God was alive, he must reveal himself to her as she was suffering through all of this. Gogo said that she believed that God did show up for her, because she had prayed that Lydia would not die in her arms and had asked that God would do something before Lydia died. That is exactly what she believed happened. God showed up through us and is now caring for her through us too. When we told her that we would support her each month for her electricity, food, clothing and school fees [through the money that Joanna had sent] she just cried and cried and said – 'My God, my God, you are alive and have heard my prayers.' Riekie continued 'Just think of it – a day that we simply do what we think is right, is actually planned and arranged by God.' And it is the saving Grace for an 'insignificant' old black woman in a township. God saw it differently. My prayer is that we will not miss what God wants to do through us for many other 'insignificant' people.

These stories reveal how much of a joy and privilege it is to be involved in the lives of the poor, who present themselves in so many different guises. We receive from them an immeasurable deposit of God's grace and we learn from them the enormous value that God places on every human life.

The Unique Value of Human Life

GOD, *investigate my life; get all the facts firsthand. I'm an open book to you; even from a distance, you know what I'm thinking. You know when I leave and when I get back; I'm never out of your sight. You know everything I'm going to say before I start the first sentence. I look behind me and you're there, then up ahead and you're there, too – your reassuring presence, coming and going. This is too much, too wonderful – I can't take it all in!*

Is there any place I can go to avoid your Spirit? to be out of your sight? If I climb to the sky, you're there! If I go underground, you're there! If I flew on morning's wings to the far western horizon, you'd find me in a minute – you're already there waiting! Then I said to myself, 'Oh, he even sees me in the dark! At night I'm immersed in the light!' It's a fact: darkness isn't dark to you; night and day, darkness and light, they're all the same to you.

Oh yes, you shaped me first inside, then out; you formed me in my mother's womb. I thank you, High God – you're breathtaking! Body and soul, I am marvelously made! I worship in adoration – what a creation! You know me inside and out, you know every bone in my body; You know exactly how I was made, bit by bit, how I was sculpted from nothing into something. Like an open book, you watched me grow from conception to birth; all the stages of my life were spread out before you, the days of my life all prepared before I'd even lived one day.

> *Your thoughts – how rare, how beautiful! God, I'll never
> comprehend them! I couldn't even begin to count them – any
> more than I could count the sand of the sea. Oh, let me rise
> in the morning and live always with you! And please, God,
> do away with wickedness for good!*

> Psalm 139:1–19, The Message

In 1967, when David Steele introduced a bill to Parliament
which eventually brought about a radial change in our
Abortion Laws, our nation took a huge step towards the
devaluing of human life. When a mother's egg and a
father's sperm come together at the point of conception, a
unique human individual begins life. Within eight days,
before a woman's period is even missed, the developing
embryo has nestled into the safety of its mother's womb.
Only days after missing her first period, the heart of her
tiny baby is already beating; two weeks later the limbs are
forming. Now visible to the naked eye, the child becomes
recognisably human. Between the sixth week of pregnancy
and the twelfth week of pregnancy all of the baby's
features develop: tiny fingers with little fingernails, the
fingers bearing a unique fingerprint, different to any other
person, even an identical twin; the mouth, the nose, the
ears and the eyes are all formed, the eyes with an iris with
a never-to-be-repeated pattern (these may perhaps form
the basis of our future security identification). Just twelve
weeks after a woman misses her period, the baby is fully
formed in almost every respect. The safe environment of
its mother's womb provides the warmth, food and oxygen
needed for the maturing of the body's systems and a safe
incubator for the next six months.

The commonest abortion procedure in this country is the
Suction Termination of Pregnancy (STOP) which dislodges
the baby from the wall of the mother's womb and sucks
it away down a plastic tube. The procedure is undertaken

usually (and most commonly) around the tenth, eleventh and twelfth week of pregnancy, removing from the mother not a 'blob of cells' but a fully formed and recognisable human child. The liberal amendments to our Abortion Laws around ten years ago meant that abortions can be performed legally right up until the twenty-fourth week of pregnancy. Children have been born alive from as early as 21 to 22 weeks. In an even more obscene amendment to our abortion laws, a baby that is considered 'severely handicapped' can be aborted right up to the time of their birth at 40 weeks. Much of the time and energy of our hospital obstetric units is spent weeding out 'the defectives' with pre-natal search-and-destroy tests and techniques. A routine ultrasound scan at 18 weeks, once called a dating scan, is now often called an 'anomaly scan'. Older mothers, who have a higher risk of conceiving a baby with Down's syndrome, are offered specific screening to preclude them from such a 'terrible event'. Similarly, many other genetic diseases can be screened for, because who would want to have a baby that is not 'normal'?

The challenge to the sanctity of human life is an enormous spiritual battle. I do not intend to go into this in great detail; as I have already stated, this is not specifically a book on abortion. However, in the context of understanding how precious the value of human life is to God, it is important to comprehend that society seems to grade and evaluate human life, deciding on quality of life before a child is born, ignoring the intimate relationship that God longs for with each person.

The beautiful Psalm of David that we now know as Psalm 139 introduces us to the intimate perspective that God has from our earliest beginnings within our mother's womb. 'For you did form my inward parts, you knit me together in my mother's womb' (13), 'my frame was not hidden from you, when I was being made in secret, intricately wrought in the depths of the earth' (15). The loving hand of God was upon each one of us in those hidden days of our lives. And yet, amazingly, we were in his eyes and heart even before we were formed. 'Your eyes beheld my unformed substance; in your book were written, every one of them, the days that were formed for me when as yet *there was none of them*' (139:16) (my emphasis). God has a plan and a destiny for each of us, whatever our race, colour, abilities, or whether we are 'normal' or 'defective'. Even before we were born, he knew our destiny. He has a longing and a yearning that we should fulfil the dreams that he has for us.

When I was conceived, I was a 'mistake'. My older brother was just five months old; the post-war years of the late fourties and early fifties were hard, and my parents were not in a position to support another child. My mother came to terms with it by deciding that I would be a girl. On the day of my birth seven children were born at the maternity hospital in Swindon, six of whom were girls. My mother was initially devastated to have borne another son but quickly became grateful to God when it was revealed that a child had been born with a disability. She says now that she has no regrets. So many people live through their life believing they are a 'mistake'. God has no mistakes; my parents may not have planned me, but God did. My days were written in his book even before that 'untimely' conception. And I was born in his *perfect* timing, the very day, the very hour of his choosing, into my family, with my parents, into this country, for such a time as this.

Many people have asked the question: 'Where does human life begin?' Biologically our lives may begin at the point of conception, and yet Psalm 139 indicates that actually our lives begin in the heart of God even before this time. Once conceived, God imparts this spirit and life into those tiny developing cells that become you and me.

The prophet Jeremiah was set apart for God even before his birth. 'Before I formed you in the womb I knew you, and before you were born I consecrated you; I appointed you a prophet to the nations' (Jer. 1:5). In Luke's gospel, we hear of Elizabeth, 24 weeks pregnant with her son John, meeting Mary bearing Jesus, 'just a few cells' in his mother's womb (Lk. 1:40–41). Baby John 'leapt for joy' in the presence of his Lord. What an amazing perception! If Mary and Elizabeth had lived in our nation today, their babies could both have been legally aborted.

The challenge to the sanctity of human life is now pressing upon us from many sides. In 1967 David Steele suggested that abortion would help do away with such social ills as child abuse and illegitimacy. And yet since that time in 1967, rather than seeing these difficulties diminish, we have seen an enormous rise in both problems. The claim that abortion would only be used in limited and defined circumstances has now led, in effect, to the policy of abortion on demand, where children's lives are destroyed on the whim of inconvenience or simply for being the wrong sex. The affront to the sanctity of human life which abortion represents started our nation down a slippery slope from a place where human embryos are created and destroyed at will, to the ever-increasing clamour for the legalisation of euthanasia. It seems that we learn nothing from history. We did nothing when the pro-abortion lobby promised that the procedure would have a limited use, merely protecting women against the evils of an illegal abortion, and yet we now have nearly two hundred thousand abortions every year in Britain (as shown in national statistics). As we now hear the incessant demands of those looking to legalise euthanasia and promising that this, of course, will be used for very 'special cases' for those suffering from terminal and debilitating disease, we need to ask ourselves how long would it take before we would be destroying the lives of people who simply are a burden to society? 'Oh this could never happen' is a common response, and yet only seventy years ago, on the continent of Europe, over six million Jews were destroyed through a programme which began through the 'kind' doctors relieving the suffering of those who were terminally ill[1] (see www.carenotkilling.org.uk).

Abortion takes away the life of the child made in the image of God and denies the world of a unique and never-to-be-repeated life. And yet even more than this, abortion often destroys the lives of women and their families. The physical harm that abortion causes women includes catastrophic bleeding, pelvic infection, (which may lead to an increase in ectopic pregnancy and infertility), subsequent premature labour, and (according to many recent research papers) an increase in breast cancer. Worse than this, women often suffer a long-term mental torment which literally changes the course of their lives. The Royal College of Obstetrics and Gynaecology, in the information that they put out on termination of pregnancy, minimises all of these problems. In their factsheet, *'About Abortion Care: what you need to know'*, the college states:

- 'If there are *no problems* with your abortion it will not affect your future chances of becoming pregnant … Your fertility *may* be affected if you have serious infection … or if you have an injury to your womb' (emphasis mine).

- 'Research evidence shows that having an abortion does not increase your risk of developing breast cancer.' (This statement implies therefore that the many papers which show a statistically significant increase in breast cancer following abortion have been ignored.)

- 'Some studies suggest that women who have had an abortion may be more likely to have psychiatric illness or self harm than other women who give birth or are of a similar age. However, there is no evidence that these problems are actually caused by the abortion; they are often a continuation of problems a woman has experienced before.'[2]

By denying that the lives of women are damaged by abortion, those who perform abortions justify their position by saying that there is no solid evidence of this damage which can be substantiated by good clinical trials. Clinical studies are difficult, if not impossible, to undertake following an abortion because, quite reasonably, women are reluctant to admit to, or even talk about their experience. They may not have even told their husband or partner that they have had an abortion. These same pro-abortion groups are not prepared to listen to the stories of women's emotional pain, dismissing these women as 'those who have often had similar problems before pregnancy', and stating that 'anecdotal' evidence does not stand up to scrutiny. The mountain of anecdotal evidence is now so huge, we simply cannot ignore it. Sometimes I feel that clinical explanations simply miss the point. It is clear to anyone who has come into contact with abortion, in any context, that it can have huge repercussions on a woman's physical and mental well-being. Ten per cent of the work of our centres is now helping women through the pain that they have suffered following abortion. It is our goal to be honest about abortion and to recognise that sometimes coming to terms with an abortion becomes a deep-rooted grieving process. Part of my vision for providing support to these women, stems from the situations I have encountered in General Practice.

Very early in my career a young woman (who had been trying to conceive a child with her husband for over a year) came in to see me. I did not know her past history as she was new to my patient list, but she did admit that she had been dogged by gynaecological problems (pelvic infection) for some time. Sensing that she may have had an abortion earlier in life I asked if she had ever been pregnant before. At this point she broke down in floods of tears and admitted to me that she had become pregnant three years earlier, without any problems at all, but that she had had a termination of pregnancy. She was now unable to conceive another child, and at the time of moving and leaving my medical list, she had not conceived.

A 'heart sink' patient came to one of my surgeries, doing the rounds of all the practice partners, with her symptoms of anxiety and depression. I decided to try to give her a little more time and simply asked her where she felt all her problems had begun. In a dramatic outburst she said 'Oh I know exactly where all my problems began. Ten years ago I had an abortion, and if I had a knife in my hand now I would stick it through the heart of the person who did that to me' (and at that point she got up from her chair and lunged towards me in a theatrical demonstration of her intended actions upon that gynaecologist).

More recently I saw a lady in surgery who was going through a period of depression and difficult time in her marriage. She seemed to bear much resentment towards her husband. They had had two children together, but both had now grown up and left home and the relationship with her husband was beginning to break down. In trying to elucidate the causes of her difficulties, she quite openly admitted that her problems stemmed from having an abortion three years before she had successfully started a family. Her husband had felt that it was too soon to have a child and had been unsupportive of the pregnancy and, hence, she had had a termination. 'Do you still think about it?' I asked. She looked up at me, and with tears in her eyes said, 'It is the first thing that I think about every single morning when I wake up.' Every morning for over twenty years of her life, her first waking thought was of her aborted child.

I have another lady on my list who has suffered a lifetime of depression and seen the breakdown of her marriage, following an abortion over twenty years ago. She now contributes regularly in a financial way to the work of the Firgrove Centre but once said to me 'If only you had been there then.'

Women who face the fear, shame and loneliness of an unexpected pregnancy are now able to come to our centres to find practical help and hope in the midst of their distressing situations. We pray that for many, our work will save them from the pain of going through an abortion and will see them choose life for their unique, beautiful child. For many other women who have been through the experience of an abortion, our centres offer post-abortion counselling through 'The Journey', a pathway of healing for broken lives (published by CARE). 'The Journey' has been a remarkable tool in the restoration of the lives of many women. Without trying to deny or bury their experience, women take responsibility for their actions, confront the humanity of the lost life, and release that life into the hands of a loving God. 'The Journey' has helped bring closure to the pain of abortion for many women, and has helped to bring them hope for the future.

Our prayer within Firgrove and Care Centres Network is that we will cover our nation with caring and compassionate Crisis Pregnancy Centres, where every woman in our country can receive help within a few miles of her home. We long to see a centre in every major town and city in Great Britain. For those women who are unable to seek help from a local centre or for those who prefer not to have a face-to-face encounter, our national helpline CARE*confidential*[3] provides access to a source of help. Although the phone line has only been operational for three years, it already receives over five hundred calls a month from women desperate for help, or from women seeking healing in their post-abortion brokenness.

During the time that we have been working in Pregnancy Counselling Centres, we have consistently been labelled as being 'Pro-life. Those people and agencies that are in favour of abortion are often labelled 'Pro-life. The views of these two groups seem to be increasingly polarised and the actions of the extremes are becoming frightening. For men and women to invoke the name of God when they burn down abortion clinics and shoot 'Pro-choice' doctors is simply abhorrent. I am sure that they may do such acts with great conviction, and yet to me, they are the acts of those who have allowed their eyes to be focused on a 'cause' (abortion), rather than have their eyes focused on God. Jesus reached out with tender compassion to the women caught in adultery, even though her crime was deserving of death. Would this same Jesus come to our abortion clinics today to burn them down and kill their doctors, or would he extend the same hand of tenderness and mercy that he offered the guilty adulteress? Yes, it is right that we should fight injustice, challenge abortion and campaign to see change, but surely we must do this with the same compassion of our Saviour who 'hated sin but loved the sinner.'

Throughout our network of centres, we have tried to get away from the polarised views of the 'Pro-life' and 'Pro-choice' lobbies. These labels are completely unhelpful.

We are certainly 'for' life, in that we respect and value the human life from its earliest beginning. And yet we are also 'for' women *and* 'for' choice, because we value and respect each woman in the same way that we respect her baby, and we recognise that each woman has the right to make her own decision. If she chooses abortion, we may be saddened by her decision, but we cannot stop loving her, valuing her, and being there for her if she so desires. This may seem strange to some of you; can we really support a woman who chooses abortion? Is not our Christian life a matter of choice? Does God force us to love him, even though eternal separation awaits those who do not? The very basis of our 'faith' rests upon the fact that we can willingly *choose* to submit our lives to the God of love. Jesus continually recognised this in his earthly ministry. In his meeting with the rich young ruler, he loved him, but allowed him to walk away rather than force him to follow. If God respects our choice, knowing that it will break his heart if we choose not to follow him, should we not also respect the choice of the woman, even if she should choose abortion? God never closes the door to anyone; he is always willing to love accept and forgive. Should our attitude not be the same?

One of the most distressing parts of our abortion legislation is the clause that says that 'an abortion may still be performed after 24 weeks of gestation if the child is found to have a "significant handicap"'. The very existence of this clause devalues a life with disability and brings affirmation to the concept of 'a life not worth living.' To me, this whole concept is absolutely obscene and my experiences in life have shown me that people with disabilities should be afforded the same value, respect and privilege as the able-bodied. They are just as unique, beautiful, clever, and talented as the able-bodied. They are perfect in God's eyes – why is 'different' seen as 'worse'?

Even as I write this, these words sound condescending, as if we should view the handicap with pity and treat them any differently to ourselves. We need to look through the 'fingers' of the disabled life, to the person whose value and worth is exactly the same as ours.

David's Story

David Anthony was born on 20 April 1951. At the age of five, whilst visiting his grandparents in Wales, he had a fall and sustained a bang to his head, which became very red and did not seem to be clearing up. His parents were concerned about this, so they arranged for him to be seen at Great Ormond Street Hospital in London and two doctors said that the bone underneath the area of bruising had thickened but there was no need to worry. If this was present as he got older he would be able to have the bone trimmed. At his home back in Lincoln, David started at infants' school, but quite quickly his teacher became concerned that he kept falling over. David was seen by a paediatrician who said there was nothing wrong with him, but again, because of his parents' concern, they asked David's GP to refer him for a second opinion. After a careful examination by a consultant paediatrician at Lincoln County Hospital, David was eventually diagnosed as having muscular dystrophy, a genetic condition passed down through the mother's line and for which there would be no hope of a cure. This distressing condition leads to progressive muscular weakness and wasting, with children soon losing their mobility, and usually progressing to death in their teenage years.

David was given physiotherapy through his infant and junior school years but, as predicted, the disease progressed, and it was obvious that he would be unable to attend a normal senior school. The nearest residential school for the physically handicapped children of Lincoln, was the Thieveswood School near Mansfield, which David could attend once he had turned twelve. There would, however, be a short period of time after leaving junior school and before attending Thieveswood that David would miss out on schooling if other arrangements were not made.

At that time my mother, who was a trained teacher, was beginning her career again after taking time out to raise her family. She began to do home teaching and was asked to take David on as one of her pupils, as we lived very close to where he lived. Through my mother, I was introduced to David and, although he was two years older than I was, we soon became close friends. My brother Richard and I would often go and play with him, having great fun racing 'Scalextrix' cars, and playing with tape recorders, pretending to be DJs.

By this time David was in a wheelchair; he was unable to walk and his arms were becoming progressively weaker. Despite his disabilities, I never once heard him grumble or complain, and he always radiated warmth and laughter. When David was twelve he started attending the Thieveswood School but would come home at weekends and during the holidays and we were soon together again renewing our friendship.

We had many common interests, going to cubs and scouts, and trips to watch our beloved Lincoln

City. David's parents were wonderfully kind and generous people and had endless patience in helping David with his disability. His father, Doug, would take David to all the Lincoln City home games, and even some of the away games, irrespective of the weather.

David enjoyed his time at Thieveswood School and greatly benefited from being there. He became a house captain and took part in numerous activities including gaining his Duke of Edinburgh Bronze Award and obtaining a refereeing certificate for football. In a school report from his head-teacher she wrote: 'In spite of his very severe disability David refuses to be downhearted. His contribution to the overall life of the school, by his sense of justice, his outstanding courage and sense of humour, is beyond praise.'

In 1967 David turned sixteen and he left Thieveswood School, returning to Lincoln where arrangements were made for him to attend a handicapped centre. It was there that he learned handicraft skills and despite his increasing disability, made a table lamp for my mother which she still has to this day. With him living back in Lincoln, we had more opportunity to be with him and to observe the amazing strength of character that he displayed in coping with this increasing handicap. Through the love and commitment of his parents, David exceeded his life expectancy, but finally succumbed to his terrible disease on 17 March 1970. I can still hear my father's voice waking me from my sleep the following morning to tell me of David's death.

At the age of sixteen, coming up to seventeen, I was entering early manhood. I knew that 'big boys don't cry', and on hearing of David's death I put on a brave face. The funeral service was held at our local church where David had been able to express his living faith. Towards the end of the service the sun broke through the clouds and I remember a sunray piercing the stained glass window and resting on David's coffin as if God was welcoming him home. Still I did not cry. After his funeral we went together to the crematorium for the final part of our service. As the curtain drew around the coffin for the final time I broke down and sobbed. I had lost my friend.

David once said to his father 'there must be a reason for people like me.' On hearing of his death, his former head-teacher from Thieveswood wrote to David's parents and said, 'It was a great privilege to have worked with you all, and *I often wonder who taught who*' (my emphasis). David's immense courage in handling his illness, his acceptance without grumbling, his ability to love and radiate joy to those around about him, enriched not only my life but everyone who knew him. I certainly learned a tremendous amount from David, of a radiant life lived in the face of great adversity, but I also learned a lot from his parents who were examples of total 'given-ness' to the care of a fragile life. More than this I have treasured memories of a person whose life has so deeply touched mine: it was simply a privilege to have known him. David was my friend.

Some years ago, I was asked to speak at a conference in the Midlands. The conference was for medical students and was organised by the Christian Medical Fellowship. The conference was highlighting many of the social issues that were facing our country, and I was asked to be a seminar speaker, addressing the issue of abortion. During my time at the conference, I met a man called Peter who was also running one of the seminars, and I struck up a rapport with him because he came from my wife's home-town of Plymouth.

One evening Peter and I were chatting together over a drink, and he began to tell me of his son, Daniel, who has Down's syndrome. Daniel was only about twelve at the time and despite his handicap, Peter told me he was capable of incredible spiritual insights. Peter told me of a time when he and his wife were counselling a couple with marriage difficulties, and Daniel came into the room; without knowing anything of the situation, he got them to hold hands.

Peter then recounted an amazing story of a time when Daniel had to go to London for an operation. Because of the difficulties with his Down's syndrome, he was admitted to Great Ormond Street Hospital and was on a surgical ward with several critically ill children. One morning while Daniel was in hospital, the porters arrived from theatre to collect a young child who was having major heart surgery that day. It had been explained to the child's mother that the chances of success of the operation were only 50:50 and that the child may even die under anaesthetic. When the porters arrived for this child the mother became hysterical and could not face relinquishing her child into the care of the hospital staff. With the tension mounting on the ward, Daniel went over to the side of the trolley and took control of the situation; 'Pray, pray!' he said and soon the ward became quiet. Daniel then prayed this prayer:

'Jesus!
Amen!'

Daniel's simple prayer broke the tension of the situation and the child proceeded to surgery. That child not only survived the operation but was healed through the surgery.

More recently I have read the remarkable true story of Martha Beck, detailing her personal journey of conceiving and giving birth to a child with Down's syndrome. The book became an American bestseller, and is called *Expecting Adam*. Martha and John Beck are Harvard graduates – intelligent, popular and parents to a perfect little girl called Katie. When Martha discovers she is pregnant with a child who has Down's syndrome, her whole life falls into disarray as she agonises over what to do. Having neither strong religious belief, nor strong views on abortion, Martha weighs up whether to keep her baby. Through the decision-making process however, she feels utterly compelled to keep her baby, despite reservations voiced by John.

> *'Look,' he (John) said. 'I know I can't always see things from your perspective, and I'm sorry about that. But the way I see it, if a baby is going to be deformed or something, abortion is a way to keep everyone from suffering – especially that baby. It is like shooting a horse that's broken its leg.' John's father had been born to a clan of sheep herders and he was always quick with barnyard analogies.*
>
> *'A lame horse dies slowly, you know?' said John. 'It dies in terrible pain. And it can't run any more, so it can't enjoy life even if it doesn't die. Horses live to run; that is what they do. If a baby is born not being able to do what other people do, I think it better not to prolong its suffering.'*
>
> *'And what is it,' I said softly, more to myself than to John, 'what is it that people do? What do we live to do, the way the horse lives to run?' I didn't expect an answer, and John didn't give one. He just moved his chair closer to mine and*

put an arm around my shoulders. 'You're awfully tired, aren't you?'

I nodded, trying to hold back another wave of tears ... John brought his other arm around and folded me to his chest. He was still wearing his bulky down parka. It was like a pillow against my cheek. I could feel his heart beating beneath the coat. For a moment I let the anxiety in my chest relax, let myself forget everything I had to do that day, let myself feel utterly safe. And then I understood that John was answering my question, even though he did not know he was. This is it, I thought. This is the part of us that makes our brief, improbable little lives worth living: the ability to reach through our own isolation and find strength, and comfort, and warmth for and in each other, this is what human beings do, this is what we live for, the way horses live to run.[4]

During her pregnancy Martha faced many difficult times, not least when she was confronted with a room full of her Harvard student peers discussing new obstetric technologies. She said that she 'particularly remembered one man leaning across the table and declaring':

'It is the duty of every woman to screen her pregnancies and eliminate foetuses that would be a detriment to society!'

At that time, I was too stunned and exhausted to do anything more than numb out. To this day I have no idea whether that particular classmate knew about my situation. I don't even remember the guy's name. But I still think about him. I thought about him when I wrote an exposé of the Harvard-trained Latin American dictator who tortured and killed thousands of political opponents. I thought about him when we all discovered that the infamous Unabomber (an American terrorist) was a Harvard man as well – a genius by all accounts.

I also thought about that seminar classmate on Adam's ninth birthday. Adam had insisted on going to a pizza-and-games arcade for his party. The only person he had invited besides his sisters was someone I'll call Lonnie, whom Adam claimed to be his girlfriend. Although I often heard Adam sing about Lonnie I had never met her, or seen Adam interact with any girl. I was afraid that he would start humping her leg the second she came into range. These were fears I had sustained since before he was born; I thought all people with Down Syndrome were grossly overaffectionate I was grossly wrong.

Lonnie turned out to be a beautiful child who had a perfectly normal brain but had been emotionally damaged by an abusive relative during the first few years of her life. She appeared timid and wary in the crowded pizza parlor until Adam rushed to stand beside her. The moment she saw him, she relaxed and broke into a shy grin. Adam had donned his best suit and tie for the occasion. He graciously took Lonnie's elbow and guided her through the pizza parlor, clearing the way in front of her with his other hand, like a cross between a professional bodyguard and a Disney version of Cinderella's prince. Lonnie's father had warned me that the rides would frighten her, and that she would probably refuse to go on them. To everyone's surprise, though, Lonnie seemed completely unafraid as long as Adam was beside her. I will never forget watching the two of them on the miniature rollercoaster, Adam's hand resting reassuringly on Lonnie's arm, their faces transported with identical, absolute joy.

Now then. If my unknown classmate from the Harvard gender seminar of 1988 is anywhere out there, I'd like to speak to him directly. I'd like to ask him to put Adam on one side of the 'screening' scale and the Unabomber on the other, and then tell me who is the 'detriment to society'. If the brilliant bomber wins out, I can only wonder, sir, exactly what kind of society you are trying to create.[5]

These moving stories, reveal to us the unique lives of beautiful people made in the image of God. To us their lives may appear to be a broken image, and yet the image of perfection that the world tries to attain to may, indeed, reveal a far lesser image than somebody with Down's Syndrome. The antenatal screening for Down's Syndrome and the subsequent termination of such pregnancies deprives us of a person made in the image of God; a person with whom we can share life, joy, compassion and faith.

At a recent Care Centres Network conference, we were privileged to have as one of our main speakers John Wyatt, the Professor of Neonatal Paediatrics and a Consultant Neonatal Paediatrician at the University College of London. Whilst at the conference John told us a story of baby Christopher, a child diagnosed with Edward's Syndrome. Christopher's story is also told in John's book, *Matters of Life and Death*.

> *Alan and Verity are close friends from my local church, All Soul's, in the heart of London's West End. My wife, Celia, and I have known them for many years and, as two couples we have shared our lives. In the spring of 1996, as we enjoyed an evening together, Verity told us that she was expecting a baby. We discussed the news with anticipation and excitement. But only two weeks later the outlook had changed. A routine ultrasound scan at 20 weeks showed major abnormalities. The diagnosis was Edward's Syndrome, a tragic and rare chromosomal disorder which causes multiple malformations, severe mental impairment and a uniformly fatal outcome. In this condition nearly all obstetricians will recommend abortion. What possible point can there be to continuing a pregnancy where there is no hope of long-term survival? Yet after agonising and heartfelt discussion Alan and Verity decided not to have an abortion but to continue with the pregnancy.[6]*

Alan and Verity chose not to have Christopher aborted. They had seen their child on an ultrasound scan and recog-nised that 'he had already become a real person and it seemed terrible to be thinking of ending a life that was already, in our opinion, so complete.' Despite the severity of Christopher's handicap they knew that they had the opportunity to be parents of a unique individual and as Verity said; 'We were able to connect with him as a human being … he communicated with us and we did with him and that ability to create a relationship with another human being is … wonderful.' Verity described how Christopher 'seemed to have the ability to draw love out of people in quite a unique way, people were able to hold him and he was a very peaceful baby and seemed to melt the coldest heart and really made people love him.' Verity would attend St Christopher's Hospice in Sydenham:

and take Christopher around the wards where people were dying. They were able to hold a baby who was also dying and in need of terminal palliative care. And somehow that shared experience between a baby who was dying and an adult who was dying was quite remarkable.

One of Verity's patients, Beatty, who was dying of leukaemia, was especially fond of Christopher and one day when I visited her she said, 'Now Christopher, I don't know who is going to die first, whether it is going to be you or me, but I will be waiting for you in heaven with my arms open ready to welcome you when you arrive.'[7]

John Wyatt continues; 'When Christopher was born he was the smallest member of the church, and when he died, seven months later, he was still virtually the same size.' A friend summed up his influence: 'Although he was unable to grow, he helped others to grow.' Christopher died in the summer of 1997. Yet his influence still carries on. I do not want to imply that there was no sadness. There was and still is a deep sense of grief and loss at Christopher's disability and untimely death.

Alan and Verity and their family and friends have known tears and heartache, and those feelings continue. But behind it all is the Christian conviction that even the weakest and most malformed human being had a life of unique value. Christopher in his way was a God-like being, a masterpiece. His life was an example of Christian theology in practice, and it was a privilege to know him.'[8]

For each one of us, whether we be 'disabled' or 'able-bodied', whatever our race or creed, whether we feel love or unloved, we all need to come to a place where we know that we are unique individuals in the eyes of God. As Psalm 139 so wonderfully explains, we were known in the heart of God even before the time of our birth. God has planned every single one of our days, and longs that we should find fulfilment by walking in the light that he has mapped out for us. The concept of the 'life not worth living' is a hideous distortion of the truth; for each one of us, our life is precious in the eyes of God. As Christians we should value and respect every God-given life, however fragile and weak and especially protect those who have no way of protecting themselves.

I love the story of Gideon found in chapter 6 of the book of Judges. The angel of the Lord 'came and sat under the oak at Ophrah, which belonged to Joash the Abiezrite, as his son, Gideon, was beating out wheat in the winepress to hide it from the Midianites' (6:11). The Midianites had been oppressing the Israelite people and God had allowed this to happen because of their disobedient and wayward lifestyle. The Midianites had come repeatedly and burned the crops of the Israelites, so that food was scarce and God's people were suffering very badly. In the midst of this scene, God visits Gideon. What I like about this story is Gideon's fighting spirit. He was determined not to be beaten down by his oppressors, and was using the winepress to hide the fact that he was rebelling against the Midianite oppression. God commends this spirit by saying 'The Lord is with you, you mighty man of valour' (6:12). Gideon questions this apparent nonsense-statement, and yet God had seen a man who was not prepared to sit back and be beaten down, but was prepared to take action. This was the valiant spirit that God looked for, when he chose a man to do a most incredible work. Gideon felt weak, unprepared and ill-equipped for the task that God had called him to, and yet in simple obedience, he not only destroyed the image of a false god, but with just 300 men, he went out and destroyed the whole army of the Midianites. Clearly the victory in the battle was a miracle of God, and yet such is God's love for us, he chooses that we should be involved with him, however small a part we may seem to play.

In the planning of the Firgrove Centre, as we took one step, God took four. As we took another step, God worked a miracle, and suddenly life became exciting. We were chasing after a God of miracles, and he graciously allowed us to be involved.

My involvement in Firgrove has taught me that, however small our contribution, we can all be involved in tackling injustice, extending mercy and reaching out to the 'poor'. I hope that in reading this book some of you may have been inspired to become involved in social action, and perhaps even work within the abortion issue itself. If your inner voice is saying: 'What, me? I could never do anything,' consider again the lives of Lord Shaftesbury, William Booth or Christine Thomas who in simple obedience considered that they could do 'something'.

During the time of writing this book, the Southampton City Council had planned to close a sports hall where I play five-a-side soccer. The sports hall is in a deprived part of town and it not only provides enjoyment to a diverse cross section of people from the city of Southampton, but it is also the focal point for many activities within the local community. The building is old and needs a considerable injection of money to maintain its continued use as a sports hall. The council had felt that such an investment was a waste and hence closure had been planned. Many of us who use the hall felt that this closure would be extremely detrimental, not only to our own lives, but to the enjoyment and general well-being of the local deprived community. We embarked upon a campaign to prevent its closure (led by an energetic care worker, Nick Chafey) and supported by many of us who also use the hall. My own involvement included writing lots of letters to local councillors and my local MP and a letter to the local evening paper (which was published), going on a protest march, and attending a 'scrutiny' meeting at the local council, where I was able to voice my concerns to a number of the local councillors. Yesterday I heard from Nick Chafey that the council had backed down and the building will be saved. It would have been far too easy to do nothing, to think, 'What can I do?' If issues are important to us, simply by being involved, we can bring about radical change.

Becoming involved in our society does not have to be limited to a particular cause or group of people. By simply responding with the right attitude to the call of the Holy Spirit, there is so much that can be achieved. The opportunities that are around us every day are endless. It is fantastic that more Christians than ever are now getting involved in political parties, being elected to sit on city councils, and even putting themselves forward to become prospective parliamentary candidates. Others have offered their services as school governors, become youth group leaders, or given their time by driving their vehicle for the use of the ambulance car service. For far too long, many of us in evangelical churches have lived out our lives within an insular and closed environment, believing that simply going to house group meetings and 'church on Sunday' was a sufficient expression of our Christian faith. It is time for Christians to 'get a life'. Our challenge is to be *in* the world but not *of* the world. We should be looking to Jesus as our example of a life filled with social action.

> *Rescue the perishing; don't hesitate to step in and help. If you say, 'Hey, that is none of my business,' will that get you off the hook? Someone is watching you closely, you know – Someone not impressed with weak excuses.*
>
> *Proverbs 24:11–12, The Message*

Choice

I

being formed in secret
mysteriously
graciously
love of a creator God
inspires my growth
my movement
cell upon cell
my life called into being
by His desire
His eyes upon my forming body
In darkness known by Him
And chosen

Christine Thomas

The God of Love

In Luke's gospel chapter 15, Jesus tells three parables relating to the 'lostness' of mankind. First we hear about a man who has lost one of his 100 sheep and rejoices when his one lost sheep is found. The second parable is of a woman who loses one of her ten silver coins and diligently cleans her house until she has found it. The last parable details the story we have come to know as the parable of the Prodigal Son. It is interesting to note the context of these parables and the fact that Jesus was speaking to the Scribes and the Pharisees:

Now the tax collectors and sinners were all drawing near to hear him and the Pharisees and the Scribes murmured saying, 'This man receives sinners and eats with them.'
... And (Jesus) said 'There was a man who had two sons; and the younger of them said to his father, 'Father, give me a share of the property that falls to me.' And he divided his living between them. Not many days later, the youngest son gathered all that he had and took his journey into a far country, and there he squandered his property in loose living. And when he had spent everything, a great famine arose in that country, and he began to be in want. So he went and joined himself to one of the citizens of that country, who sent him into the fields to feed swine. And he would gladly have fed on the pods that the swine ate; and no one

*gave him anything. But when he came to himself he said,
'How many of my father's hired servants have bread enough
to spare, but I perish here with hunger! I will arise and go
to my father, and I will say to him, 'Father, I have sinned
against heaven and before you; I am no longer worthy to
be called your son; treat me as one of your hired servants.'
And he arose and came to his father. But while he was yet
at a distance, his father saw him and had compassion, and
ran and embraced him and kissed him. And the son said to
him, 'Father, I have sinned against heaven and before you;
I am no longer worthy to be called your son.' But the father
said to his servants, 'Bring quickly the best robe and put it
on him; and put a ring on his hand, and shoes on his feet;
and bring the fatted calf and kill it, and let us eat and make
merry; for this son was dead, and is alive again; he was
lost and is found.' And they began to make merry.*

*'Now his elder son was in the field; and as he came and
drew near to the house, he heard music and dancing. And he
called one of his servants and asked him what this meant.
And he said to him, 'Your brother has come, and your father
has killed the fatted calf, because he has received him safe
and sound.' But he was angry and refused to go in. His
father came out and entreated him, but he answered his
father 'Lo, these many years I have served you, I have never
disobeyed your command; yet you never gave me a kid, that
I might make merry with my friends. But when this son of
yours came, who has devoured your living with harlots,
you killed for him the fatted calf!' And he said to him, 'Son,
you are always with me, and all that is mine is yours. It
was fitting to make merry and be glad, for this your brother
was dead, and is alive; he was lost, and is found.'*

Luke 15:1–2 and 11–32

Last year I was asked to speak in a seminar, during one
of our church meetings, on the issue of compassion. After
the seminar a young man came up to me and presented

me with a tape by Dwight Pryor and this tape introduced me to the work of Kenneth Bailey, which I have previously referred to. In his book *Poet and Peasant*, Kenneth Bailey gives a fascinating insight into the background of this parable, and it is through these insights that we are able to discover the enormity of the compassion and the love of God.

For over 15 years I have been asking people of all walks of life from Morocco to India and from Turkey to the Sudan about the implications of a son's request for his inheritance while his father is still living. The answer has almost always been emphatically the same. As I have noted elsewhere the conversation runs as follows:

'Has anyone ever made such a request in your village?'
'Never!'
'Could anyone ever make such a request?'
'Impossible!'
'If anyone ever did, what would happen?'
'His father would beat him, of course!'
'Why?'
'This request means – he wants his father to die!'

In the literally hundreds of times I have asked the question, 'Do you know of anyone who has made such a request?' only twice did I receive a positive answer. In the first case Pastor Viken Galoustian of Iran, with a convert church of Oriental Jews, reported to me that one of his leading parishioners, in great anguish, reported to him, 'My son wants me to die!' The concerned pastor discovered that the son had broached the question of the inheritance. Three months later the father, a Hebrew Christian (a physician) in previously good health, died. The mother said 'He died that night!' meaning that the night the son dared to ask for

his inheritance the father 'died'. The shock to him was so
great that life was over that night. In a second case a Syrian
farmer's older son asked for his inheritance. In great anger
his father drove him from the house.[1]

By opening the parable with the words of a son requesting
his inheritance from his father, Jesus would have captured
the attention of the listening Scribes and Pharisees. Imagine
the scene: an unheard of action is vocalised, the forbidden
thought spoken out in public, audible gasps emanate from
the listening crowd. In effect, the son was saying 'I wish
you were dead'; that amounts to a total rejection of his
father, and a humiliation in the presence of family and
friends. It is surprising that the father even consents to
such a request.

As we follow the story through we see the younger son
squandering all of his money in a far-off country. He has
not only rejected his father but seems to have rejected the
customs, the values, and faith by which he was raised. He
spent his money on 'loose living' and 'devouring his living
with harlots.' When faced with poverty, he even became
a pig herder, tending animals considered unclean within
the Jewish faith. Desolate and hopeless, the son comes to
his senses, and decides to return to his father, with a face-
saving gesture to ask to become one of his 'hired servants'.
The youngest son had recognised the folly of his ways and
yet he believed the way back to a relationship with his
father was to become a worker for him and, through his
own efforts, pay back what he owed.

The central tenet of the Christian faith is that there is
absolutely nothing that we can do to work for, or attain
to, our own salvation. Unlike other religions, Christianity
has revealed the true nature of the God of love, a God
who reaches down with compassion and grace and freely
bestows salvation and a restored relationship on those who

return to him. As Jesus recounts this parable he reveals the father heart of God to each one of us.

Kenneth Bailey continues:

> *The Oriental farmer and landowner lives in his village, not in isolation out on his land, this has always been the case ...*
>
> *Most likely the father expects the son to fail. He is assumed dead. If he makes it back, it will be as a beggar. The father also knows how the village (which certainly has told him he should not have granted the inheritance in the first place) will treat the boy on his arrival. The prodigal will be mocked by a crowd that will gather spontaneously as word flashes across the village telling of his return ... As soon as the prodigal reaches the edge of the village and is identified, a crowd will begin to gather. He will be subject to taunt songs and many other types of verbal and perhaps even physical abuse.*[2]

So the scene is set for the return of the prodigal son. Here we see a father actively looking out on a daily basis desperately hoping that his son will return. Put yourself in the place of the father – imagine not seeing your child for months, not knowing whether they are alive or dead, wondering whether you will see them again or whether they even care. And then a speck appears on the horizon. You dismiss it, as you always do and rub your eyes. The speck turns into a figure and your heart begins to race. The forlorn figure takes on the familiar shape of someone you used to know and you can barely contain your joy ... And yet this father had no reason to be joyful with a son who had humiliated him and wanted him dead. Nevertheless, abandoning all reasoning and propriety, the man, while his son was still a long way off, *ran* to embrace him.

This act of the father has further significance when we set the story in the context of the customs of the day. In eastern culture it is actually very undignified for an elderly man to run. And yet in order for his son not to face the humiliation from the locals that his return should rightly bring, the father humiliates *himself* by *running* to meet his son. His actions convey a heart so full of love, so overcome by joy that he simply longs for reconciliation – regardless of the humiliation that he may suffer. Such was the amazing love that he had for his child that he sought to avert the judgemental eyes and the condemnatory voices of the onlookers by degrading himself.

Again Jesus uses the amazing 'compassion' word, *splagchnizesthai*. The father was filled with gut-wrenching compassion for his son, a compassion which had already allowed him to do the unthinkable in releasing his son's inheritance; a compassion which caused him to be looking out for his son on a daily basis; and a compassion which caused him to humiliate himself in the eyes of the world, in order to bring his son into a reconciled relationship. And yet the father's love didn't end here. The father demands that the best robes be brought and placed around his son, indicating his total acceptance in the eyes of the community. He places a ring on his finger to signify trust and places shoes on his feet, a sign of his son being a free man within his father's house. Finally the killing of the fattened calf was a sign that a banquet was about to be held: the whole community would be invited to enjoy the feast that would be laid on.

This parable, in just a few short verses, encapsulates the message of the whole gospel of Jesus Christ. We sin, doing things to hurt God and other people. We are selfish, pleasing ourselves before others. If we are humble enough to recognise that we have made a mess of our lives, we sometimes think that we can make things better and earn our salvation by doing something for God. And yet as we draw close to God, and come back to him in repentance, we find a father who has humiliated himself further, through the death of his son on the cross and, in rejecting our worthless offerings, bestows salvation upon us freely and without reserve. This salvation is a salvation of joy, a banqueting feast, an eternal embrace with the father. Heaven explodes with celebration when one person repents and turns back to God.

From my earliest teaching within the Christian church, I can concur with Henri Nouwen, who says; 'I realise that I am not used to the image of God throwing a big party, it seems to contradict the solemnity and seriousness I have always attached to God. But when I think about the way in which Jesus describes God's Kingdom, a joyful banquet is often at its centre.' The whole essence of a restored and reconciled life is to discover the sense of joy that God wants to place at the centre of his relationship with us. It is amazing that we so often find prayer difficult. Perhaps this is because we have a false notion of God as being a severe father simply waiting to chastise us when we set a foot wrong. Whereas God will discipline his children in love, Jesus has revealed to us a God who is passionate about each of us and longs that we should all come into his presence and talk with him. In his book, *Reflections for Ragamuffins*, Brennan Manning writes:

> We pray so little, so rarely, and so poorly. For everything else we have adequate leisure time. Visits, get-togethers, films, football games, concerts, an evening with friends, an invitation we can't decline – these are good because it is natural and wholesome that we come together in community. But when God lays claim to our time, we baulk. Do we really believe that he delights to talk to his children? If God had a face, what kind of face would he make at you right now?
>
> Would his face say, 'When are you going to pull yourself together? I am fed up with you and your hang-ups. My

patience is exhausted. We are going to have to do a little reckoning'? If God said only one word to you, would the word be *Repent*? Or would he say, 'Thank you. Do you know what a joy it is to live in your heart? Do you know that I have looked upon you and loved you for all eternity?' What would God say? What is the feedback you get from your creator?[3]

The most important journey of our lives is to learn how to have a deep and intimate relationship with our loving Father. Everything else is peripheral, temporary, and merely a signpost along the way to this intimate relationship with God.

My understanding of the immense love of God has been helped through my involvement with Care Centres Network. I have already spoken of our relationship with South Africa Cares for Life, and of our friendship with Riekie Van De Berg. Some years ago Riekie told us an amazing story which reveals the incredible love of God.

Sarah's Story

One evening a young 'Cape coloured' South African girl was coming home from a party. On her way home she was grabbed by three black men and taken to a hut in their township where she was chained to a bed and repeatedly raped by these three, and a fourth man. For over three and a half months this young girl was imprisoned and repeatedly gang raped until she was eventually found by the police. The police took the young woman to Riekie, in her capacity as social worker running a pregnancy crisis centre, in order to have a pregnancy test. Legally, she could have had an abortion and the police were expecting that Riekie would help sort this out. The young woman was filthy and naturally looked terrible. Whilst doing the pregnancy test Riekie was able to explain to her the choices that now confronted her and was able to share the contents of Psalm 139 – that God had a purpose and a plan for her life and (if she was pregnant) a plan for her unborn child. The young woman was very moved by the thought that God could be involved in her life. The pregnancy test proved to be positive. Riekie explained that when she was raped she was subject to a violent act over which she had no control or choice, but now Riekie explained to her that she could take control again of her life and make a choice that suited her.

The young woman listened to Riekie's words expressing God's love and felt secure in being unconditionally accepted. She made the decision to stay at the centre and not to go with the police to the hospital for an abortion. Riekie said, 'It was not my counselling, but God's presence and grace that touched her heart.'

Although the young woman was not a Christian, as Riekie shared with her and loved her she made a simple commitment to God. She had chosen to continue with the pregnancy but, as she neared the end of her pregnancy, she felt that she would not be able to look after her baby. She therefore asked Riekie to find adoptive parents for the child. For Riekie this presented a seemingly impossible situation. The mother was a young mixed race girl and the father would have been black. The child would be mixed race, and in South Africa no couples would want to adopt a mixed-race child.

Riekie prayed about the situation and then shared about it in her church meeting, and wrote about the dilemma that she faced in the church newsletter. There was no response. Riekie then asked the young mother to join her in trusting God for an answer to prayer and ask God to show her what to do. The young mother who had so recently given her life to God did not know how to pray. 'What do I say?' Riekie was able to teach her to pray a very simple prayer in faith and to expect God to answer her, perhaps through other people, perhaps through a dream, or in a way of God's choosing.

After a few days the young mother came back to Riekie and explained that she had had a dream. In her dream she had given birth to a little baby girl, but she could not look after her. She then found herself by the side of a river, where the riverbank was all stony, and as she felt that she could not look after her baby she felt compelled to throw her baby in the water. Just before throwing her daughter into the river, she heard somebody calling to her from the other side of the river: 'Throw your baby to us.' Looking up, she saw a tall man and a short blonde woman. They were calling to her, asking her to throw them her baby daughter. Her dream continued, and she threw the baby across the river to the couple on the other side. She could see that the bank of the river on the other side was green and lush unlike the stones on her side of the river, and in her heart she knew her baby would have a good life. After she had thrown her baby to the couple on the other side of the river, the river began to get wider and wider; soon it became a vast ocean and the couple disappeared. The young girl then awoke from her dream.

Coming back to Riekie she asked, 'What does this dream mean?' Riekie had no idea.

During this same period of time, a couple in Riekie's church went on a retreat a couple of hours drive out of the city of Pretoria. At a meal table during the retreat, they shared with other people around the table how Riekie was looking for an adoptive family for a difficult-to-place child. Coincidentally, at the same table were a couple whose son and daughter were on holiday with them, having just arrived from the United States. This couple were childless and had been praying for a child to adopt. Through a word from God, they were told to go to South Africa, where they were to adopt a child that 'nobody else wanted'. Riekie's friends from the church gave them Riekie's phone number so that this couple could make contact.

Riekie arranged a meeting and through the door came a tall man and a short blonde woman! Initially Riekie tried to convince them that she had no white babies for adoption but the couple explained they had come for the child that no one else wanted. Riekie then called the young woman in to the meeting and she saw the couple from her dream! Together they spent the afternoon crying and talking about the faithfulness of God. With the birth of the young mother's child just two weeks away, the couple were able to stay in South Africa and were present at the time of the birth.

Giving birth to her child the young mother immediately looked at the sex of the baby – a little girl. As she held her daughter in her arms, she said; 'How could anything so beautiful come from something so wicked?' She then went on to name the four men who had raped her and, before those present in the room, she forgave them. In an act of great courage, she then gave her baby daughter, Sarah, to her new adoptive parents.

Following her adoption, Sarah's parents became missionaries in the Philippines. They were also able to adopt a second child from Riekie, a little brother for Sarah. Sarah's father wrote to Riekie some time ago to say that he had been having difficulty getting through to the Philippine people. One morning he felt God guide him to simply walk through the village with his family and not to wait at the church building as they had normally done.

Our two children ran on ahead (as children do) and I saw other children join them. Sarah called me over. She said, 'Daddy, the children asked why I am black and you are white. I told them I have a miracle story if they want to hear it – so come and tell them.' I sat down on the dirt road and told the children Sarah's story – that God can change your circumstances and make good come out of bad. Some of the children got up and walked away – but only to go and call their parents to hear the story! Later more parents joined us and that day I was able to lead most of the village people to faith in Christ.

This amazing story of Sarah from Riekie's work in South Africa teaches us many things. The story is miraculous and speaks of redemption and forgiveness, of hope and of faith. But the thing that amazes me most of all from Sarah's story is this. Out of *six billion* people in the world today, how can God love one poor 'insignificant' child so much, that he organised the lives of so many people in order to bring about such joy, such redemption? Out of the midst of such evil, God directed the lives of the police, the young woman, Riekie, Riekie's church friends, the missionary couple, and their parents, all for the joy of redeeming one poor mixed race and 'unwanted' child conceived in violence, bitterness and hate. Such is the boundless and immeasurable love of God. It is to this God that we come, the God who runs to welcome us; the God who trusts us and accepts us, just as we are; the God who prepares a banquet for us because he is so happy that we have returned to a relationship with him. It is into the intimate arms of our father, that we commit ourselves in the final chapter.

10

There's something about Mary

> *Now as they went on their way, he entered a village; and a woman named Martha received him into her house. And she had a sister called Mary, who sat at the Lord's feet and listened to his teaching. But Martha was distracted with much serving; and she went to him and said, 'Lord, do you not care that my sister has left me to serve alone? Tell her then to help me.' But the Lord answered her, 'Martha, Martha, you are anxious and troubled about many things; one thing is needful. Mary has chosen the good portion, which shall not be taken away from her.'*
>
> *Luke 10:38–42*

I have to say that, as a young Christian, when I first read the story of Mary and Martha, I felt exceedingly sorry for Martha. It seemed to me that she was doing the right and polite thing in preparing a meal for Jesus and her friends and was simply being a good hostess. I have always thought it was harsh that she seemingly received such a rebuke from Jesus, whilst apparently commending the 'laziness' of her sister Mary. My understanding of the story merely reflected the immaturity of my walk with Christ and perhaps reflected fundamental values of society which had infiltrated my very existence. Speaking to others about this story I found that many people have similarly found

Jesus' actions harsh. I think the people who have the most difficulty with this story are the 'achievers', the people who have lived their lives 'doing' rather than just 'being'.

From her years as a trained counsellor, my wife tells me that there are different ways we can understand people's behaviour. We can either be 'through-time people' or 'in-time people'. Through-time people are always looking to achieve the next thing in life, looking to the future, planning, and yet, perhaps, missing the joys of the moment; in-time people are never really bothered about what may happen tomorrow, but recognising that we must live each day moment by moment, experiencing the fullness of God in the present.

It may seem in writing this chapter that I am commending that we should become in-time people but this is not really the case. I think that the ideal we find in Jesus is a combination of both characters. I have always lived my life much more as a through-time person and I have needed to bring my life back into balance in order to experience the joy of the 'now-moment' and to discover a place of true intimacy in my relationship with Christ.

As with all facets of Jesus' nature, he seemed to hold these tensions in perfect harmony. Not only does he commend Mary for discovering this 'in-time' moment, but in the lengthy passage from the Sermon on the Mount, he tells us not to worry about tomorrow and what it may bring, but rather let each day take care of itself (Mt. 6:25-34). However, because Jesus knew of an intimate relationship with his Father on a day by day basis, he was able to 'set his face to go to Jerusalem' (Lk. 9:51) planning for his future (being through-time) and his ultimate sacrifice.

The busy nature of our lives and the fast pace of modern society often demands that we live 'through-time'. In doing so, we can miss out on the fullness of each day, causing us to have no time for reflection and intimacy with God. The actions of Mary in sitting at Jesus' feet, spending time with him, and listening to him, are the actions of one who was discovering true intimacy. These were the actions that Jesus commended. Mary's desire for intimacy represents the kind of relationship that God wants with each of us.

The New Testament gives us three beautiful stories about the life of Mary and Martha. In John's gospel chapter 11 we are told the story of the death of Lazarus, the brother of Martha and Mary. Lazarus had been very ill and so Martha and Mary had sent for Jesus who had been delayed in his coming (11:6). On hearing that Jesus was eventually arriving in their village, the impetuous Martha jumped up and ran for two miles out of the village to meet him. Questioning why it had taken Jesus so long to come, she greeted him with words, 'Lord if you had been here, my brother would not have died' (11:21). Mary did not go with her sister. As Jesus and Martha drew closer to the village, we are told that Martha went to Mary and said to her: 'The teacher is here and is calling for you.' It was only on hearing these words that Mary 'rose quickly and went to Him' (11:29).

The sisters had clearly been talking about Jesus' delayed arrival, because when Mary came into the presence of her Lord she also said: 'Lord if you had been here, my brother would not have died' (11:32). The interesting thing to note however is the different attitude of the two women in coming into the presence of Jesus. Martha had rushed out to meet him and her action of running the two miles to confront him perhaps displayed her grievance that he had not come sooner. On the other hand Mary waited until Jesus called her and, on coming to him, she fell at his feet and wept. It was when Jesus was confronted with these actions of Mary that he was deeply moved. Jesus wept.

There are only two occasions in the recordings of the New Testament that we find Jesus weeping. He wept over Jerusalem, and the fact that the city was lost (Lk. 19:41), and he wept when confronted with Mary in her hour of grief. It seems strange that Jesus would be weeping over the death of Lazarus, as he already knew that 'this illness is not unto death; it is for the glory of God, so that the son of God may be glorified by means of it' (11:4). There was something about Mary that reduced Jesus to tears. He had not been so moved when confronted by Martha, who had greeted him with the very same words that Mary had spoken to him. Could it be that the intimacy that Mary discovered was the very thing that caused Jesus to be moved with such empathy?

In the following chapter of John's gospel, Jesus came back to Bethany, just before the feast of the Passover. With Lazarus now raised from the dead, Jesus entered his home to have a meal with him. The busy, bustling Martha was, once again, preparing the meal. With his disciples and Lazarus seated around the table, Mary comes to Jesus and, in an amazing act of worship, took a very costly ointment and anointed his feet. The ointment was of pure spikenard, anointing oil that was only used in burial rites. With Jesus just days away from his death, Mary had perceived the hour.

Even though his disciples had been with him now for three years, none of them was aware of the significance of this moment; not Peter, James or John, his closest friends; or Martha, whom he loved, bustling in the kitchen; and not Lazarus whom he had raised from the dead. Though all these people had been profoundly touched by Jesus and had walked with him during his journey to the cross, it was Mary who came to him at this momentous hour, and anointed his feet with the oil of burial. It was to Mary that God gave this divine revelation, and in Matthew's account of this same story, Jesus tells us that, 'Wherever this gospel is preached in the whole world, what she has done will be told in memory of her' (Mt. 26:13).

The alabaster jar of pure nard was incredibly expensive, probably worth a year's wages for the average labourer. By today's wage rate, perhaps worth ten to fifteen thousand pounds. An alabaster jar was the best possible vessel for maturing the oil, like the ageing of a fine wine in an oak cask. When Mary came to Jesus she broke the jar and anointed him with this oil, causing gasps amongst his disciples. They were indignant that she had seemingly 'wasted' such an expensive and costly commodity. This rare oil from India was traditionally only used in burial. Why did Mary have the oil in the first place? It could not have been for her brother Lazarus. He had died once already; he had been anointed before being raised from the dead. Could it have been that this oil was for her? Was she keeping it for her own burial?

Just as we often make provision for our own funerals, perhaps she had made provision for hers. The fact was, the oil was hers to give, and she came and gave all that she had. She even wiped the feet of Jesus with her hair. Her hair was her glory, not to be let down in front of a man. But Mary came, and let down her hair, and wiped ointment into the feet of Jesus. His dirty feet! Her beautiful hair was now covered in oil and grease, matted, dirty and difficult to wash out; highly perfumed, she would have been covered with the scent of death. In the intimacy of her relationship with Jesus, not only had God entrusted her with divine revelation, but in an act of her own free will she had come and given extravagantly, laying aside her dignity, foregoing her future security. What a contrast to the reaction of his disciples! It was not only Judas who baulked at the wastage; Matthew recalls 'when the *disciples* saw it, they were indignant, saying, why this waste? For this ointment might have been sold for a large sum and given to the poor' (emphasis mine) (Mt. 26:8–9).

The life of Mary gives us a beautiful picture of intimacy with Jesus. Mary teaches us that 'the better place' is to be in the presence of Jesus. She chooses this over the bustling busyness that the world demands. Mary teaches us of the trust and confidence we can have in our Saviour, of the adoration and love that we can give to him and, amazingly, how this love, adoration and trust can move his heart. It is to such people that God entrusts his revelations that may have eternal consequences. Inspired by the life of Mary, Ken Gire wrote a beautiful poem, which is found in his wonderful book, *Windows of the Soul*.

Broken Vases

The aroma of extravagant love.
So pure. So lovely.
Flowing from the veined alabaster vase
of Mary's broken heart –
A heart broken against the hard reality
of her Savior's imminent death.
Mingled with tears, the perfume became –
by some mysterious chemistry of Heaven -
Not diluted but more concentrated,
Potent enough behind the ears of each century
for the scent to linger to this day.
Doubtless, the fragrance, absorbed by his garment,
as it flowed from his head,
Accompanied Christ through the humiliation of his trials,
the indignity of his mockings, –
the pain of his beatings,
the inhumanity of his cross.
Through the heavy smell of sweat and blood,
A hint of that fragrance must have arisen
from his garment –

Until, at shameful last, the garment was stripped
and gambled away.
And maybe, just maybe, it was that scent
amid the stench of humanity rabbled around the cross,
that gave the Savior the strength to say:
'Father, forgive them, for they know not what they do.'
And as Mary walked away from the cross,
The same scent probably still lingered in the now-limp hair
she used to dry the Savior's feet –
A reminder of the love that spilled
from his broken alabaster body.
So pure. So lovely.
So truly extravagant.
It was a vase he never regretted breaking.
Nor did she.[1]

A life of intimacy with Jesus begins by sitting at his feet, listening, praying. Having been a Christian 38 years I have found the discipline of prayer one of the most difficult things within the Christian life. I must have sat through countless sermons, read numerous books, and attended many seminars and yet I have not found praying something that has come naturally to me. I have been helped tremendously by a story related by Brennan Manning in his book, *Abba's Child*.

Once I related the story of an old man dying of cancer. The old man's daughter had asked the local priest to come and pray with her father. When the priest arrived, he found the man lying in bed with his head propped up on two pillows and an empty chair beside his bed. The priest assumed that the old fellow had been informed of his visit. 'I guess you were expecting me,' he said.

'No, who are you?'

'I'm the new associate at your parish,' the priest replied.

'When I saw the empty chair, I figured you knew I was going to show up.'

'Oh yeah, the chair,' said the bedridden man. 'Would you mind closing the door?'

Puzzled, the priest shut the door.

I've never told anyone this, not even my daughter,' said the man, 'but all my life I have never known how to pray. At the Sunday Mass I used to hear the pastor talk about prayer, but it always went right over my head. Finally I said to him one day in sheer frustration, 'I get nothing out of your homilies on prayer.'

'Here,' says my pastor reaching into the bottom drawer of his desk. 'Read this book by Hans Urs von Balthasar. He's a Swiss theologian. It's the best book on contemplative prayer in the twentieth century.'

'Well, Father,' says the man, 'I took the book home and tried to read it. But in the first three pages I had to look up 12 words in the dictionary. I gave the book back to my pastor, thanked him, and under my breath whispered "for nothin".'

'I abandoned any attempt at prayer,' he continued, 'until one day about four years ago my best friend said to me, "Joe, prayer is just a simple matter of having a conversation with Jesus. Here's what I suggest. Sit down on a chair; place an empty chair in front of you, and in faith see Jesus on the chair. It's not spooky because He promised, 'I'll be with you all days.' Then just speak to Him and listen in the same way you're doing with me right now."'

'So, Padre, I tried it and I've liked it so much that I do it a couple of hours every day. I'm careful though. If my daughter saw me talking to an empty chair, she'd either have a nervous breakdown or send me off to the funny farm.'

The priest was deeply moved by the story and encouraged the old guy to continue on the journey. Then he prayed with him, anointed him with oil, and returned to the rectory.

> *Two nights later the daughter called to tell the priest that her daddy had died that afternoon.*
>
> *'Did he seem to die in peace?' he asked.*
>
> *'Yes, when I left the house around two o'clock, he called me over to his bedside, told me one of his corny jokes, and kissed me on the cheek. When I got back from the store an hour later, I found him dead. But there was something strange, Father. In fact, beyond strange, kinda weird. Apparently just before Daddy died, he leaned over and rested his head on a chair beside his bed.'*[2]

Just as this man had recognised that he could simply talk to Jesus as if he was sitting in the chair opposite, I have often envisaged Jesus sitting in the passenger seat of my car as I drive to and from work. Much of our life is spent doing things that allow us to come into the presence of God if we simply refocus our attention to him. So instead of turning the radio on as I drive to work, I try instead to talk to Jesus, as if he were my passenger and driving with me. We must learn to develop the attitude encouraged by Brennan Manning, so that when we come into the presence of God we hear him say 'Thank you; I have been waiting for this, I've got so much to share with you.'

When I first started envisaging Jesus as my passenger, I began to try and listen to what he was saying to me in response to my prayers. Driving to work one morning, I was praying about my work for the day, and I was asking that Jesus would simply use me in whatever way he chose. Immediately in my mind I had the thought of an elderly woman, who had been 'harassing' me the previous five years because of an intractable pain that she was experiencing. We had performed every investigation known to medical science; she had seen three different consultants, and yet she still came in to see me week after week complaining of this pain. It seemed that there was nothing that I could do for her.

At the surgery we now work a new system of booking appointments called 'Advanced Access' and this means that patients do not generally book advanced appointments but simply ring the surgery on the day of their illness, in order to be seen that day. I was not aware, therefore, who I was likely to be seeing that day and it was with some surprise that I found this elderly woman was booked for my first appointment of the day. One of the things that I am learning about prayer is that we cannot bring our petitions to God if we are not prepared to be involved in his answer. Surely it could not be a coincidence that this woman had come to my mind as I started praying about my day's work, and then for me to arrive at surgery and find her booked first on the list.

I sometimes find it difficult to broach the area of faith with patients, as clearly that is not my primary responsibility, and neither should I use my position as a GP to intrude spiritually into people's lives uninvited. However, having nothing else to offer this lady medically, I simply asked her if she had a faith and if she had ever considered praying about her intractable pain. She stated that she did have a faith but had never prayed about her pain. However she consented to me praying with her that God would intervene on her behalf. I wish I could say that God dramatically healed her, but I do not believe this was the case. What I do know however, is that when I finished praying for her, she was weeping, having sensed the love of God touch her life. I have certainly seen her far less in surgery since that time, but I do not yet know what will be the final outcome with regard to her pain. In a sense though, that is not my problem.

In our relationship of intimacy with God, we discover that *we* have certain responsibilities and God has certain responsibilities.

I cannot ever 'make' anybody a Christian; salvation is a gift which only God can bestow. But I can love people, show compassion to people, and share my faith with them when the opportunity arises. I can never heal anybody. (Even as a doctor, one of the first things I learned was that I would never, ever heal anybody, but I may help to bring the right conditions to a human body so that it may heal itself.) Similarly if I pray for healing, I cannot bring about that healing work. That is God's responsibility; but I can pray, and respond to the whispers of God in our intimate moments.

From the lives of the saints who have gone before us, we can discover that our day to day living can be a reflection of a life of true intimacy. Mother Teresa wrote:

> There are some people who, in order not to pray, use as an excuse the fact that life is so hectic that it prevents them from praying. This cannot be. Prayer does not demand that we interrupt our work, but that we continue working as if it were a prayer. It is not necessary to always be meditating, nor to consciously experience the sensation that we are talking to God, no matter how nice this would be. What matters is being with him, living in him, in his will. To love with a pure heart, to love everybody, especially to love the poor, is a twenty-four-hour prayer.[3]

Through the work of the Firgrove Trust and Care Centres Network I have discovered that the goal of my journey is a place of true intimacy with God. I believe the reason abortion grieves the heart of God, is because it not only denies the world of a unique and never-to-be-repeated individual, but it denies God of the passionate and intimate relationship that he wants to have with one of his children. The call to social action, to becoming involved, has opened my eyes to the amazing grace, the gut-wrenching compassion, and to the infinite and abounding love of God. As we are drawn towards this love, we discover a place of true intimacy; we then find that we come full circle, and find new expression of the life of Jesus through our generosity to others. Our involvement in social action is not through duty or blind obedience, but it is simply a lifestyle that we learn by sitting at the Master's feet.

The hideous and wicked acts of the September 11th plane hijackings ushered the world into a new dark era of terrorism and hatred. The increasing number of terrorist atrocities, 'the wars and rumours of wars', the hunger, the famine, the starvation; the AIDS epidemic and the terror of new diseases such as SARS and variant CJD, the breakdown of family values and the degeneration of our society: all these things can lead us to despair, and the sense that the world is about to end. In the midst of this despair God speaks: 'You are the salt of the earth' (Mt. 5:13). As God's people there is an opportunity for us to 'preserve' the world and 'stay the hand of God'.

The Times article of October 16 2001, which followed the atrocities of September 11th in the United States, was actually written by Peggy Noonan in November 1998, three years *prior* to the murderous events of that day. Her article predicted terror attacks in the United States, but far more importantly, it identified the basis of our hope.

I once talked to a man who had a friend who had done something that took his breath away. She was single, middle-aged and middle class, and wanted to find a child to love. She searched the orphanages of South America and took the child who was in the most trouble, sick and emotionally unwell. She took the little girl home and loved her hard, and in time the little girl grew and became strong, became, in fact, the kind of person who could and did love others. Twelve years later, at the girl's High School graduation, she won the award for the best all-round student. She played the piano for the recessional. Now she is at college.

The man's eyes grew moist. He had just been to the graduation. 'These are the things that stay God's hand', he told me. I did not know what that meant. He explained: 'These are the things that keep God from letting us kill us all.' So be good, do good. Stay his hand. And pray … Pray! Pray unceasingly! I, myself, don't but I think about it a lot, and sometimes pray when I think … Pray unceasingly. Take the time.[4]

When the Son of Man comes in his glory, and all the angels with him then he will sit on his glorious throne. Before him will be gathered all the nations, and he will separate them one from another as the shepherd separates the sheep from the goats and he will place the sheep at his right hand, but the goats at the left. Then the king will say to those at his right hand, 'Come, O blest of my Father, inherit the kingdom prepared for you from the foundation of the world; for I was hungry and you gave me food, I was thirsty and you gave me drink, I was a stranger and you welcomed me, I was naked and you clothed me, I was sick and you visited me, I was in prison and you came to me.' Then the righteous will answer him, 'Lord, when did we see you hungry and feed you or thirsty and give you a drink? And when did we see you a stranger and welcome thee, or naked and clothe thee? And when did we see thee sick or in prison and visit thee?' And the king will answer them 'Truly, I say to you, as you did it for the least of one of these my brethren, you did it to me.'

Matthew 25:31–40

Endnotes

Chapter 2

The information in this chapter about the Earl of Shaftesbury comes from John Pollock's *Shaftesbury: The Poor Man's Earl* (Oxford: Lion Publishing, 1990).

1. Yancey, P., *What's So Amazing About Grace?* (Grand Rapids, MI: Zondervan, 1997), 11. Copyright © 1997 by Philip D. Yancey. Used by permission of The Zondervan Corporation.

2. Stott, J., *New Issues Facing Christians Today* (London: HarperCollins, 1999), 23–24.

3. Christenson, L., *Social Action – Jesus Style* (Minneapolis: Bethany Fellowship Inc., 1976), 9.

4. From *Living Parables* (The Shaftesbury Society, 2003), 3

5. Pollock, J., *Shaftesbury: The Poor Man's Earl* (Oxford: Lion Publishing, 1990), 23.

6. Battiscombe, Georgina, *Shaftesbury: A biography of the 7th Earl 1801–1885* (Constable, 1974), 334.

7. Quoted on the front cover of Pollock, J., *Shaftesbury: The Poor Man's Earl*. The original quote appeared in *The Times* newspaper.

8. Stott, J., *New Issues Facing Christians Today* (London: HarperCollins, 1999), 5.

9. Pollock, J., *Shaftesbury: The Poor Man's Earl* (Oxford: Lion Publishing, 1990), 155.
10. Stott, J., *New Issues Facing Christians Today* (London: HarperCollins, 1999), 8.
11. Christenson, L., *Social Action – Jesus Style* (Minneapolis, MN: Bethany Fellowship Inc., 1976), 17.

Chapter 3

1. *The Times* newspaper, 1981.
2. Noonan, P., *Stay God's Hand* (London: *The Times* newspaper, T2, 16.10.2001), 2. Used with permission.

Chapter 4

1. Nouwen, H., McNeill, D. P., Morrison, D. A., *Compassion* (London: Darton, Longman & Todd, 1999), 13.
2. Chesterton, Gilbert K. *St Francis of Assisi* (Garden City: Doubleday Image Books, 1957), 96–97.
3. Cahill, T., *Desire of the Everlasting Hills* (New York: Doubleday, 1999), 185.
4. Manning, B., *Ruthless Trust* (London: SPCK, 2002), 169.

Chapter 5

1. Bailey, K., *Poet and Peasant* and *Through Peasant Eyes* – combined edition (Grand Rapids, MI: Wm. B. Eerdmans, 1983), 143.

Chapter 6

1. Yancey, P., *What's So Amazing About Grace?* (Grand Rapids, MI: Zondervan, 1997), 67.
2. Yancey, P., *What's So Amazing About Grace?* (Grand Rapids, MI: Zondervan, 1997), 175.

3. Extracts from the film *Patch Adams* (Universal Studios).

4. Manning, B., *Abba's Child* (Colorado Springs, CO: NavPress, 1994), 71–72. Used by permission of NavPress – www. navpress.com All rights reserved.

5. Yancey, P., *What's So Amazing About Grace?* (Grand Rapids, MI: Zondervan, 1997), 166–68.

6. Manning, B., *Abba's Child* (Colorado Springs, CO: NavPress, 1994), 131. Used by permission of NavPress – www.navpress.com All rights reserved.

Chapter 7

The information in this chapter about Mother Teresa comes from Spink, K., *Mother Teresa: An Authorised Biography* (London: HarperCollins, 1998).

1. Spink, K., *Mother Teresa: An Authorised Biography* (London: HarperCollins, 1998), 258.

2. Manning, B., *Ruthless Trust* (London: SPCK, 2002), 168.

3. Mother Teresa, *In My Own Words*, compiled by José-Luis González-Balado (London: Hodder & Stoughton, 1997), 16.

4. Mother Teresa, *The Joy in Loving*, compiled by Jaya Chaliha and Edward Le Joly (London: Hodder & Stoughton, 1997), 317.

5. Spink, K., *Mother Teresa: An Authorised Biography* (London: HarperCollins, 1998), 123–24.

Chapter 8

1. www.carenotkilling.org.uk

2. Information from *About abortion care: what you need to know is* available on the Royal College of Obstetrics and Gynaecology website http://www.rcog.org.uk (August 2005).

3. The number for the CARE*confidential* freephone helpline is 0800 028 2228. For more details see www.careconfidential.com.
4. Beck, M., *Expecting Adam* (New York: Berkley Books, 2000), 134–36.
5. Beck, M., *Expecting Adam* (New York: Berkley Books, 2000), 238.
6. Wyatt, J., *Matters of Life and Death* (Leicester: IVP, 2000), 165.
7. Wyatt, J., *Matters of Life and Death* (Leicester: IVP, 2000), 166.
8. Wyatt, J., *Matters of Life and Death* (Leicester: IVP, 2000), 166.

Chapter 9

1. Bailey, K., *Poet and Peasant* and *Through Peasant Eyes* – combined edition (Grand Rapids, MI: Wm. B. Eerdmans, 1983), 161.
2. Bailey, K., *Poet and Peasant* and *Through Peasant Eyes* – combined edition (Grand Rapids, MI: Wm. B. Eerdmans, 1983), 180–81.
3. Manning, B., *Reflections for Ragamuffins: Daily Devotions* (London: SPCK, 2003), 8.

Chapter 10

1. Gire, K., *Windows of the Soul* (Grand Rapids, MI: Zondervan, 1996), 167–68. Copyright © 1996 by Ken Gire, Jr. Used by permission of The Zondervan Corporation.
2. Manning, B., *Abba's Child* (Colorado Springs, CO: NavPress, 1994), 126–27. Used by permission of NavPress – www.navpress.com. All rights reserved.

3. Mother Teresa, *In My Own Words*, compiled by José-Luis González-Balado (London: Hodder & Stoughton, 1997), 7.
4. Noonan, P., *Stay God's Hand* (London: *The Times* newspaper, T2, 16.10.2001), 2.